Day*walkS

Cannock Chase

a network of 35 linked footpath routes
exploring the sandy hills and valleys
over the whole of the Chase.

by John Roberts
with sketches by Liz Johnson

****
WALKWAYS
J S Roberts
8 Hillside Close, Bartley Green
Birmingham B32 4LT
****

DaywalkS: Cannock Chase
(Second Edition)

ISBN 0 947708 28 6

First Published 1987   ISBN 0 947708 16 2

WALKWAYS

DaywalkS Footpath Networks

Arden   Chaddesley Woods
Clent & Lickey Hills   Elan Valley
Vale of Llangollen   Wyre Forest

The first four are currently in folded A2
sheet format, sold in a plastic cover.

Strolls & Walks

From each of about twenty places there is a
stroll of a mile or so and a walk of 4 or 5 miles.

Strolls & Walks from Picnic Places (Midlands)
Strolls & Walks from Cotswold Villages
Strolls & Walks from Midland Villages

Long Distance Routes

Step by step guides in both directions which
often connect with each other and Long Distance
Footpaths. (A2 sheets folded to A5,
but Heart of England Way is a book.)

Llangollen to Bala   Bala to Snowdon
Birmingham to Ludlow   Ludlow to Rhayader
Rhayader to Aberystwyth
Birmingham to Church Stretton
Heart of England Way

8 Hillside Close, Bartley Green, Birmingham B32 4LT
(Send sae for current list & prices.)

To enjoy the best of the countryside

Join The Ramblers.

Explore the many hundreds of thousands of miles of Britain's beautiful footpaths and receive our exclusive Yearbook full of information on walking and places to stay.

Plus regular colour magazines and newsletters — free of charge.

You will also be entitled to valuable discounts at outdoor equipment shops.

And at the same time you will be helping us to protect the countryside and to look after Britain's footpaths.

For further information and an application form, drop a line to:

The Ramblers' Association, 1-5 Wandsworth Road, London SW8 2XX

(ii)

ASSOCIATION OF
FRIENDS OF CANNOCK CHASE

The Friends aim to protect the Chase from industry and housing, to conserve its landscape, plants and creatures and preserve its unique heathland character for ordinary people.

Threats from mining, forestry, gravel digging, the Army and RAF, lead in 1934 to an original group, but the present Association started in 1947. They have objected to the M6 running over the Chase, helped to map footpaths, commented on County plans and management schemes, removed conifers, laid out deer fodder in hard winters, planted oaks and put up nest boxes. They have programmes of rambles, talks, social and natural history events and heathland management.

The Friends are affiliated to the British Deer Society, Council for the Preservation of Rural England, Staffordshire Wildlife Trust, the Staffs Industrial Archaeology Society and rambling groups. They laise with the county and district councils, the Forestry Commission and local landowners.

You could join to give them your support, and buy their booklets on the deer, industrial history and transport history.

Secretary:
Trevor Warburton, 29 Stonepine Close, Wildwood
Stafford ST17 4QS

Contents

Mixed with the boring old route directions ("Go L at the old mill etc") is a sort of bran tub of information about the Chase. A bran tub has no index and the contents is not highly organised, but its more fun that way. To make the best of it get one of the County Council's picture maps such as "Discovering Cannock Chase".

Introduction

DaywalkS networks have been around since 1986
when Bridgnorth, Kinver, Stourport came out,
followed by Wyre Forest and Cannock Chase. Although
the first one was a book, I produced the next six
on A2 sheets because they were comparatively quick
to complete and cheap to produce.

This new edition of Cannock Chase includes all the
improvements that I have taken up since the early
days. There are numbered and lettered paragraphs
for the directions which are in a distinct type
face, sketch maps for which the sheets had no
space, pictures, and a lot more information about
the walks and the countryside.

I am very grateful to the Friends of Cannock Chase
who helped with this book. You can find out all
about them on page (iii). They provided masses of
information about the geology, history, industry
and transport of the Chase, spotted my spelling
mistakes and things and tested a large sample of
the walks. Any remaining errors are mine. The
Friends are a small organisation who have done
invaluble work for the Chase over many years. They
are the only voice of the public to protect and
protest and insist, and deserve the support of
anyone who likes Cannock Chase.

The Landscape

Features on the geology, plants and creatures,
military, industrial and general history of the
Chase appear all through this book. This is an
introductory sketch to give a general picture of
the landscape and what kind of walking it promises.

The Chase covers 17,000 acres (26 square miles) and forms a kidney shaped plateau raised above the general level of surrounding Staffordshire. The Trent Valley to the north and east of the Chase is about 200 feet above sea level, a rough average for the Chase would be 450 feet. The high points are Stile Cop in the south east at 670 feet, Castle Ring on the southern tip at 780, Rifle Range Corner in the centre at 670, the Boulderstone in the north west at 630 and the East trig point at 650.

The ground is sandy gravel, dumped by the great glaciers as they melted in a warming climate about 10,000 years ago. Look out over the open heath from say, the Boulderstone and you can see how it was made from great heaps of material, as if delivered to a builders yard by monstrous tipper lorries.

If you regard the Chase as one solid block it is cut through completely in only one place. The valley of the insignificant looking Rising Brook between Cannock and Rugeley, which carries the A460 and the railway. It may not look much, but the Rising Brook may have served the world's first blast furnace at Slitting Mill.

The northern third of the Chase has small steep hills. Three main valleys cut south to north towards the Trent, Sher Brook, Abrahams and Oldacre in order of size. On the rest of the Chase the valleys and streams run east, again to the Trent, the Stoney Brook, Rising Brook and Shropshire Brook.

The southern two thirds has more massive domed hills than the north, but not much less steep. There is a terrific drop just east of Stile Cop. The map will show you that the southern Chase has been cut away by the Cannock urban area, because the Hednesford Hills and Gentlshaw Common are obviously part of the same structure.

The north has open heath and there is more in the centre, separated by a half mile belt of conifers. Their removal would be the single greatest improvement that could be made to the Chase. The heath areas have heather, bilberry, bracken and silver birch and belong to Staffordshire County Council. The rest belongs to the Forestry Commission who have planted mainly Corsican and Scots Pine and it is managed as commercial forest. Often the Pines are quite majestic and exitingly alpine; in places there is a pleasing fringe of beech on the edges of blocks.

The whole of the Chase proper and some of the outlying fragments are an Area of Outstanding Natural Beauty, and there are several Sites of Special Scientific Interest. (Anthropologists studying the lovers?)

There are fallow, muntjac and red deer, badgers, foxes and squirrels, adders and lizards. With the brooks and pools, little green glades, high points and views, rolling sandy hills and pebbly tracks, the Chase offers fine varied walking, and usually dry underfoot.

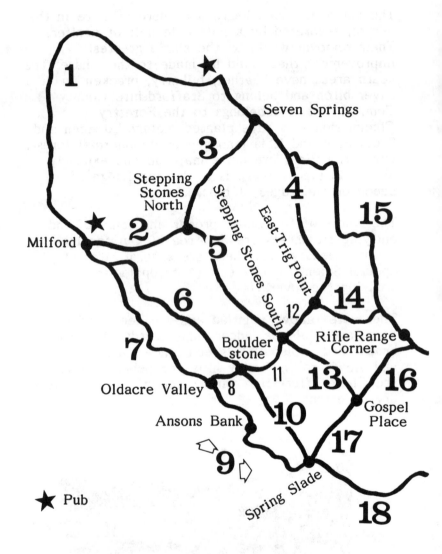

Seven Springs

1

3

Stepping
Stones
North

2

Milford

4

15

Stepping Stones South

East Trig Point

5

6

14

7

12

Boulder
stone

Rifle Range
Corner

Oldacre Valley

8

11

13

16

Ansons Bank

10

Gospel
Place

9

17

★ Pub

Spring Slade

18

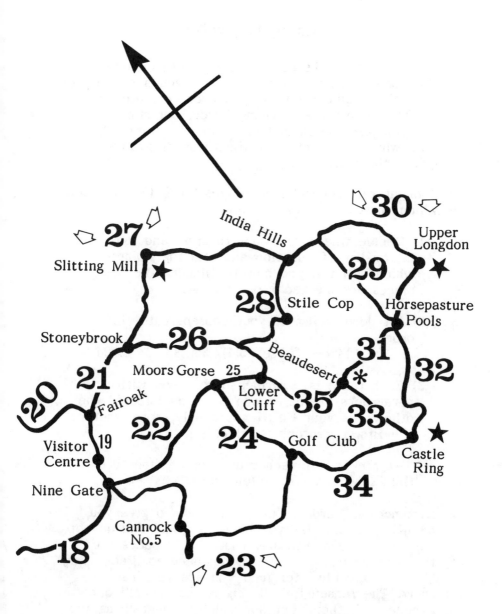

Using Daywalks

DaywalkS networks do something quite complicated as walking books go, which is to give you a whole area to explore. Like a car, telphone or computer, there are lots of pipes and wiring inside, but similarly, you can just use them and ignore the works. Just take what you want from the route directions and ignore the rest.

Look at the General Map (Pages (4) & (5) and decide which routes you want to walk:

(1) Decide where you want to start and look it up in the list of Junction and Starting Points which will tell you how to find it. The best places are marked * on the list.

(2) Jot down a list of your chosen routes in order
   Eg Moors Gorse 25(1), 35, 33, 34 & 24

(3) Each route is described both ways, with paragraphs numbered one way and lettered the other. For your FIRST route only, note whether the first paragraph is (1) or (a).

(4) At the end of each route your options are shown, so you just follow them.

Distances in yards or miles are just to give you an IDEA of how far you need to walk. You do not have to try and measure. Distance in paces are there to be counted out, if you need to. Paces vary but you can allow for it if you are very tall or short. The reason for all this is that people carry a pace with them, but not usually a measuring tape, and very few of us have really got a clue how far 200 yards is.

Amendment Service

This note is standard to all my walking books and sheets. It is less relevant to the Chase than elsewhere, but the general principle remains. The countryside changes all the time. You will meet new tracks, stiles and barns; hedges vanish and paths are diverted. To keep directions as up to date as possible I issue amendment slips.

IF you write to tell me of any changes or problems that you meet, stating route and paragraph number, I will refund your postage.

IF you send me a stamped addressed envelope with a note of what publication(s) you have, I will send you up to date amendment slips. (Phone enquiries welcome; 021 550 3158)

Transport & Information

Most people will travel to the area by car and drive to one of the Starting Points. But you can come by bus to;

	Service
Milford and Seven Springs	Stafford - Tamworth
Cannock No5 and Moors Gorse	Cannock - Rugeley
Castle Ring	Cannock - Lichfield

For up to date and detailed information on buses phone 0785 223344.

I point out whether parking space is available at each Starting Point. If you use grass verges or other odd spots, park with great care;

USE a car park wherever possible
NEVER obstruct narrow lanes
ASSUME that field gates WILL be used.

(7)

Staffordshire County Council have produced leaflets about the Chase generally, the First World War Army camps, charcoal smelting, and more. The Friends of Cannock Chase have published booklets on transport history, industrial history and the deer. Messrs C J and GP Whitehouse have published detailed histories of the Chase during both World Wars. All of these can be seen and bought from the Visitor Centre, Marquis Drive.

You will need

* A MAP
The Chase is awkwardly split between two Ordnance Survey Landranger (1.25ins/1mile) sheets, numbers 127 Stafford & Telford and 128 Derby & Burton upon Trent.

For people who are nutty about maps I give the numbers of the relevant Pathfinder (2.5ins/1mile) sheets, but their position is even worse. Apart from being nutty, the Chase occupies four maps. SJ82/92 Stafford, SK02/12 Abbots Bromley (a corner only), SK01/11 Rugeley & Lichfield (North) and SJ81/91 Cannock (North)

Save money and make do with a road atlas or the County Council's picture map "Discovering Cannock Chase", to get to your starting points. You will be safe enough or the tame old Chase. In any case, it is covered in meandering little paths which do not appear on the maps.

* CLOTHING & GEAR
Yes of course. What I meant was, suitable clothing for walking. Your own experience will be the best guide in the long run, but if you have none consider these points.

(1) Boots. Most people seems to prefer them at most times of year; go for the lightest that you can find. Trainers are excellent in dry weather and very adequate for the Chase.

(2) Socks. You don't necessarily need two pairs, but a good thickness of woolly padding is a great comfort. The traditional grey rough wool "rag sock" is hardwearing and reasonably thick, but that is about all. Try loop pile socks.

(3) Gaiters are good news in bad weather, and can keep you comfortable through mud, flood and undergrowth, not that you will meet much of these on the Chase. You can keep them on in all but the hotest weather.

(4) Jeans are cut too close for comfortable walking. Denim may be fine in California where it was first used by a Mr Levi to make working trousers, but here it is hot in summer, cold in winter, holds the damp and is in any case heavy and stiff. In summer try polycotton trousers which are light and dry in no time. In colder weather corduroy is not bad.

(5) Take a waterproof, preferably hooded and long enough to reach down to your gaiters.

(6) Take a hat and gloves and something to keep out the wind such as a showerproof jacket. Your waterproof would do, but they can be sweaty and uncomfortable. Always carry an extra sweater.

(7) In all seasons I suggest a long sleeved cotton shirt which opens all down the front. You can wear it open or buttoned to various degrees, or not at all, with sleeves rolled up or down, inside or outside your trousers, and have ventilation or protection from sun, wind, vegetation, insects, as required.

This is general advice based mainly on ordinary clothing. Visit a good outdoor equipment shop and see if they have anything to offer which would improve your comfort. For example, windproof garments and magic vests which do not stay wet like cotton T shirts. First though, try ordinary clothes to find out whether and how they could be improved upon.

Correct walking books always say that you should carry a compass and be able to use it. (If you can use one, you probably always do carry it!) But you don't need a compass on the Chase.

Rights of Way & Obstructions

DaywalkS routes are on public rights of way or well established paths and tracks. They may be Foot -paths, Bridleways or Byways (usually green lanes or tracks) with some stretches of ordinary road. Your rights as pedestrian are the same on all, you are entitled to follow the track or cross the land. The fact that it is "private" land (most land is) is quite irrelevant.

Occupiers of land are legally obliged not to obstruct paths, it is an offence, but sometimes they do. Paths should not be ploughed up nor have crops growing over them, nor should you meet barbed wire fences. You are entitled to cross or remove any such obstacles doing as little damage as you reasonably can. You may diverge to pass the obstacle so long as you go no further than is necessary and do not enter someone else's land.

Almost all the routes in this network on Cannock Chase are completely clear and will remain so, since they are on open access non agricultural land owned by the County Council or Forestry Commission. However, there are a couple of

excursions outside the Chase and there was one
minor obstruction which I hope will be dealt with
soon. And you might like to keep the above in mind
for your other walking.

The Ramblers Association and other more local
footpath and amenity groups have an important role
in keeping footpaths open. The RA has Footpath
Secretaries for each area who monitor the state of
paths, respond to closure and diversion proposals
and organise maintenance. If you use footpaths it
seems right that you should support them. See
their advert on page (ii).

Birches at Spring Slade

Junctions & Starting Points

The places are listed alphabetically to help you find the start of your walk. Once there you can follow the directions and will not need the list again. The names are taken from the nearest place that has a name, which may be at some distance.

The place I have called Lower Cliff is shown on the map as Seven Springs, but I could not use that a second time for obvious reasons.

Many Junction Points on the Chase are only accessible on foot and these are shown. You could start from them but will probably find it easier from one of the recommended Starting Points, marked * on the list.

Each Point is described and has a map reference so you can find it on a map and get there by road. The OS maps explain how to use map refernces but you can probably find most places without them.

* Anson's Bank   SJ 977171
        signposted layby car park north of Military
        Cemetries on minor Cannock - Stafford (via Pye
        Green) road.

Beaudesert   SK 039139
        crosstracks in woodland, no road access.

* Boulderstone   SJ 980181
        big rock on plinth near white trig point. Stands
        by lane (not shown on map) off minor Cannock -
        Stafford (via Pye Green) road, just north of
        (signposted) Anson's Bank car park.

* Cannock No.5   SK 009142
   industrial estate (Cannock Chase Enterprise
   Centre) on north side of A460 Cannock - Rugeley
   road. Car park and cafe.

* Castle Ring   SK 045126
   iron age fort on southern tip of Chase north of
   Cannock Wood. Car park, pub.

   East Trig Point   SJ 994180
   white trig point at five track junction where
   heath meet forest. No road access.

   Fairoak   SK 009160
   crosstracks by pond in valley, no road access.

   Golf Club   SK 029136
   bridleway passes waiting area by first tee. No
   parking.

   Horsepasture Pools   SK 050139
   crosstracks by wrought iron gates between two
   pools. No road access.

   India Hills SK 044156
   junction of tracks on ridge. No road access.

   Lower Cliff   SK 031147 (aka Seven Springs)
   T junction of tracks by pool. No road access.

* Milford   SJ 976211
   open green space at junctions of lanes with A513
   Stafford - Rugeley road by gates of Shugborough
   Hall. Pub, cafes, shops, wc's, car park.

* Moors Gorse   SK 024151
   layby and car park by waterworks on A460 Cannock
   - Rugeley road. Picnic place.

* Nine Gate   SK 004150
   car park and picnic area (map shows "Brindley
   Valley") on minor road diverging north from A460
   just north of Hednesford.

   Oldacre Valley   SJ 976182
   crosstracks in dry valley. No road access.

* Rifle Range Corner   SJ 999168
   car park (named Penkridge Bank) 250 yds east of
   Rifle Range Corner on minor Penkridge - Rugeley
   road.

* Seven Springs   SK 004205
   car park and picnic site on south side of A516
   Stafford - Rugeley road.

   Gospel Place   SJ 989166
   crosstracks in valley by forest edge at
   approximate source of the Sher Brook. No road
   access.

* Slitting Mill   SK 030171
   pool off minor road just west of Rugley which
   joins A460. Pub. Use PUBLIC (not pub) car park.

   Spring Slade   SJ 979164
   cafe by minor Cannock - Stafford (via Pye Green)
   road north of Military Cemetries. No parking.

   Stepping Stones North   SJ 988201
   crossing of Sher Brook at crosstracks on edge
   of oak and beech area. No road access

   Stepping Stones South   SJ 988178
   crossing of Sher Brook at crosstracks on open
   heath near edge of pine forest. No road access.

* Stile Cop   SK 039152
   trig point and car park at edge of forest on
   first lane south from A460 out of Rugeley.

Stoneybrook   SK 018164
stepping stones at crosstracks in valley. No
road access.

Upper Longdon   SK 058144
track meets road opposite seat in village south
east of Rugeley. Limited parking.

* Visitor Centre   SK 006153
car park and picnic site at Marquis Drive on
minor road diverging north from A460 just north
of Hednesford.

List of Routes

All routes are described in both directions, so Route (1) might have been called "Seven Springs - Milford".

Directions at some Starting Points may seem repetitive, pedantic or just plain odd. They are to cater for people joining the route at that spot, to whom I can't say "Go L" until they are facing the right way.

You may see mysterious and apparently useless information, such as "ROUTE 28 (India Hills) runs L". This is because the southern ends of Routes (26) and (28) share the same paths for about a quarter of a mile. A walker coming along (26) from Stoneybrook intending to take (28) might not want to go to the end of (26), and then retrace their steps. In fact they might say rude things. The rule is - if you don't want to know, ignore it. You will know what information is useful.

Route	Miles	Kms
(1) Milford - Seven Springs	3.7	6.0
(2) Milford - Stepping Stones N	1.25	2.0
(3) Seven Springs - Stepping Stones N	1.25	2.0
(4) Seven Springs - East Trig Point	2.2	3.5
(5) Stepping Stones N - Stepping Stones S	1.4	2.3
(6) Milford - Boulderstone	1.8	3.0
(7) Milford - Oldacre Valley	1.8	3.0
(8) Boulderstone - Oldacre Valley	.3	.5
(9) Spring Slade - Oldacre Valley (via Anson's Bank)	1.5	2.5
(10) Boulderstone - Spring Slade	1.0	1.8
(11) Boulderstone - Stepping Stones S	.7	1.1
(12) Stepping Stones S - E Trig Point	.5	.7

(13)	Stepping Stones S - Gospel Place	.8	1.4
(14)	Rifle Range Corner - E Trig Point	1.0	1.6
(15)	Seven Springs - Rifle Range Corner	3.0	5.0
(16)	Rifle Range Crnr - Gospel Place	1.0	1.6
(17)	Spring Slade - Gospel Place	.6	1.0
(18)	Nine Gate - Spring Slade	2.5	4.0
(19)	Nine Gate - Fairoak (via Visitor Centre)	1.0	1.5
(20)	Rifle Range Corner - Fairoak	1.0	1.6
(21)	Fairoak - Stoneybrook	.6	1.0
(22)	Nine Gate - Moors Gorse	1.4	2.3
(23)	Nine Gate - Golf Club (via Cannock No.5)	3.0	5.0
(24)	Golf Club - Moors Gorse	1.25	2.0
(25)	Moors Gorse - Lower Cliff	.6	1.0
(26)	Lower Cliff - Stoneybrook	1.7	2.8
(27)	Stoneybrook - India Hills (via Slitting Mill)	2.5	4.0
(28)	Lower Cliff - India Hills (via Stile Cop)	1.8	3.0
(29)	Horsepasture Pools - India Hills (West Route)	5.0	2.5
(30)	Horsepasture Pools - India Hills (via Upper Longdon)	2.3	3.7
(31)	Horsepasture Pools - Beaudesert	.75	1.2
(32)	Castle Ring - Horsepasture Pools	1.1	1.8
(33)	Castle Ring - Beaudesert	.9	1.5
(34)	Castle Ring - Golf Club	1.8	3.0
(35)	Beaudesert - Lower Cliff	.9	1.5

Sample Circuits

Start	Routes		
Rifle Range Cnr	14(1)-12-13-16	3.3	5.3
Boulderstone	8-9-17-13-11	3.9	6.3
Milford	2-5-11-6	5.1	8.3
Castle Ring	34(1)-23-19-21-26-35-33	9.9	16.0
Nine Gate	18(1)-10-6-2-3-4-14-20-19	13.0	21.0
Milford (Outer Circuit)	1(1)-15-20-21-27-30-32-34--23-18-9-7	25.0	40.0

Britain in the Age of Museums

A winding wheel from Silverdale Colliery stands
on the site of West Cannock No5 pit, now a small
industrial estate. (Route 23)

Main Map Symbols

Starting point   ●

Path or track

Stone track

Road/lane

Railway

Canal (lock)

Stream

Rivers, lakes & ponds

Edge of woodland

Building   ■

Car park   □

Trig. point   △

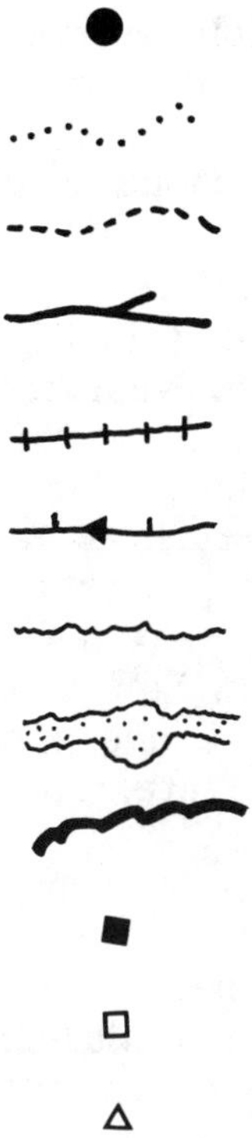

Pubs on general map only

These maps are sketches to confirm
where you are rather than for route finding.

Approximate scale
1.5 miles/1 inch   2.3 cms/1 km

1

Milford - Seven Springs
3.7 miles 6 kms

This route follows two canals, you cross the River
Trent twice and the Sow once and will probably
see sleek trains with coloured stripes, hurling
busy people about at important speeds.

The Staffordshire & Worcestershire Canal starts at
Great Haywood Junction and winds south west to the
River Severn. Near the junction the canal spreads
into the broad lake of Tixall Wide, fringed with
bullrushes and anglers. The Trent & Mersey Canal
passes the Staffs & Worcs on its way south east.
From the lock near the junction, step aside to see
the narrow Essex packhorse bridge and the meeting
of the Rivers Sow and Trent. There is a also
railway bridge and a cast iron bridge which
carried a private road from Shugborough Hall.

The Hall was built in 1693 but remodelled twice in
the next century, in my view with no better luck.
It is the home of Lord Lichfield (of Photography)
and the County Museum. The park is famous for a
whole series of dottily romantic stone follies.

Essex Bridge

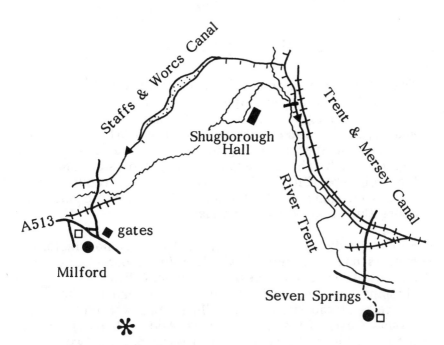

Staffs & Worcs Canal

Trent & Mersey Canal

Shugborough Hall

River Trent

A513

gates

Milford

Seven Springs

＊

Milford to Seven Springs

(1) From gates of Shugborough, (far side of common from cafes), take lane off A513 & cross river to canal.

(2) Go R on towpath appx 1.7 miles to canal junction.

(3) Take towpath R, pass lock & iron bridge & on 1 mile to next bridge by twin power poles.

(4) Leave canal & go R on lane to A513. Take track opposite to car park.

Seven Springs
●
>> OPTIONS <<
Routes 3(1), 4(1) or 15(1)

＊

Seven Springs to Milford

(a) From car park, exit to A513. [GREAT CARE] Take lane opposite to canal.

(b) Go L on towpath appx 1.5 miles to canal junction.

(c) Go L on Staffs & Worcs appx 1.7 miles, past lock, to next bridge (106).

(d) Go L on lane to A513 at

Milford.
●
>> OPTIONS <<
Routes 2(1), 6(1) or 7(1)

.... the story so far .....

The Chase is a plateau of round gravelly hills
formed in the last Ice Age, which ended some
10,000 years ago. In a warming climate plant life
and especially trees became established. The
selection of species that grow in particular places
depends on height and exposure, types of soils and
local climate. On the Chase you would certainly
have seen some of the heather, bilberry, birch and
Scots Pine that are there today.

People gradually moved north as life became viable,
hunters and gatherers slowly learning about
agriculture and permanent settlements. Flint
chippings are the earliest evidence of man on the
Chase, and the sites where flints were worked
around Castle Ring and Cannock Wood. There is no
natural flint to be found near the Chase, but we
know that there was a trade in unworked nodules
which could be manufactured locally. The two
ancient roads that cross the Chase, Blake Street
and South (or Sow) Street, were probably used
for trading in flints and salt.

The Iron Age fort of Castle Ring at about 800 feet
is the highest point on the Chase. There are five
ramparts on the less steep southern side and one
fronting the Chase, all enclosing eight acres.
Because of the view it commands and the ease with
which access could be controlled it must have been
defensible. However the functions of these
structures is not totally clear. Some may have been
used for permanent settlement but others may just
have been a refuge in times of danger. Small forts
on waterless hills seem likely to have been the
latter, but there is water in the Ring (at least,
there is now) and one can imagine a small village
there.

The Romans seem to have kept clear of the Chase, which would have had no strategic military purpose. They passed it by to the south on Watling Street, the modern A5, though there were forts at Wall just south of the Chase, and Penkridge to the west. The Romans called the tribe that inhabited the Chase the Cangi, strange so that many British tribes in those days were Italian.

Anglo Saxon tribes entered Staffordshire in the late 700's, probably keeping to the lower ground. Around the Chase there were setlements at Bednall, Acton Trussell, Brereton and Armitage.

The Domesday Book of 1086 describes the Chase as waste lands and records no settlements. It was part of the ancient Forest of Cank, which was the largest woodland mentioned at 54 square miles. The Normans extended the original wildwood by plantings to promote deer hunting and applied the draconian Royal Forest laws. By 1286 the Forest boundaries ran from Stafford down the Penk Valley in the west through Wolverhampton, Bilston, Wednesbury, Lichfield, Tamworth, Alrewas, Rugeley and back to Stafford. It therefore included areas which are still recognisably heath or woodland today, such as Whittington Heath, Druids Heath, Bentley Heath, Barr Beacon, Hints Woods and Hopwas Woods.

The small Cistercian Abbey of St Mary's was founded in 1130 at Radmore, about a mile south of Castle Ring. The monks stayed only 20 years until they were granted new land at Stoneleigh in Warwickshire. There is a nunery called St Mary's Abbey at Colwich just north of the Trent, but there is nothing now left of the old Abbey except traces of the well.

The Norman (Royal Forest) Chase included nine manors or "hays", Gailey, Teddesley, Ogley, Cheslyn, Bentley, Alrewas, Hopwas, Cannock and Rugeley. The term survives of course in the modern names of Cheslyn and Ogley Hay. There is also Boney Hay but we are not quite clear how that fits in. In 1290 the manors of Cannock and Rugeley were sold to the Bishop of Lichfield by Richard I to raise cash for the crusades. They were withdrawn from the Royal Forest and the area became the Bishops Chase, the first reference to the name. He had residences at Beaudesert and Shugborough.

With the dissolution of the monestaries, Henry VIII handed over the Bishop's rights to Sir William Paget, whose decendents became Marquises of Anglesey, and he lived in Beaudesert Hall (demolished 1935). Marquis Drive was built across the Chase to take the family from their home to the hunting in Sherbrook Valley.

Disaforestation continued until Tudor times. Deer Parks were established at Wolseley, Teddesley, Hatherton, Hagley, Beaudesert and Shugborough, the names still appear on the map. In 1560 the Pagets were licenced to fell timber to fuel their iron smelters and foundries, such as the one at Furnace Coppice and at Slitting Mill near Rugley. I cover the disgusting tale of the Pagets and the destruction of the Chase later. The outcome was that most of the oaks were cleared before the next century. Grazing sheep cut down any oak seedlings, so preventing the woodland from regenerating, and their numbers and lack of management caused erosion of the thin acid soil, so creating the heathland.

During the next two centuries the Chase was a barren waste with nothing to exploit, while coal and iron were worked to the south and east.

Photographs taken by soldiers training on the Chase in the Great War (1914 - 1918) show a treeless waste. The detailed story of the Army camps is told in "A Town for Four Winters" by CJ & GD Whitehouse, I give an inept summary later. The state of the landscape is illustrated when the authors compare the soldiers photographs of various places, only identifiable through great skill and knowledge, with their own modern ones. The Chase must have seemed barren beyond hope.

The Forestry Commission came on the scene in 1920 with a remit to grow a strategic reserve of timber. On their land in the south and east of the Chase they truly planted the best that the ground would support, Scots and Corsican Pine, with some Lodgepole Pine and Larch. More recently they have put in Sitka Spruce. One may disagree with the density of trees (there are sound forestry reasons for it), the monoculture and the regimentation. But anyone who wishes for the past should have a look at the soldiers' photos from the Great War.

Gravel extraction became important between the wars, and there are now gigantic craters at Bevins Birches on the east side and Pottal Pool in the south west. Worked out quarries at Brocton and Milford have been left to develop as nature reserves. Chase gravel is the biggest, finest quality and most easily worked supply in Europe. The scale of the danger to the Chase can be imagined if you go and see what has happened at Bevins Birches (directions below), and picture the craters full to the brim with ten pence pieces.

During World War II the RAF ran a training camp at what is now the Marquis Drive Visitor Centre. It was more compact than the Great War camps, but after the war the military still wanted to keep hold of 2,440 acres. In 1950 the Ministry of Transport wanted to run the M6 over the Chase.

In 1955 the Earl of Lichfield gave some 2000 acres to Staffordshire County Council to be preserved for public access and nature conservation. In 1958 the Chase was designated an Area of Outstanding Natural Beauty and in 1973 four and a half square miles in the north became a Country Park.

Perhaps the repulsion of the M6 was some sort of watershed, because it now seems the threats to the Chase are being held more at bay. But remember what happened at Twyford Down, an AONB near Winchester in the path of a motorway. It is being bulldozed as I write. When the Forestry Commission is sold off, will we still have free and open access to the forest sections of the Chase?

[To see Bevins Birches Quarry: follow Route (15) to para (8) or (d). Take track with quarry fence on your L past the flagpole (unless red flag is up) & walk through quarry. Return the same way.]

Gatehouse to Shugborough Hall

2 Milford - Stepping Stones North
1.25 miles   2 kms

The Stepping Stones are through the Sher Brook
which rises about three miles south at the centre
of the Chase. For a well drained sand and gravel
heath, quite a lot of water gathers in a short
distance. But because of the way in which the
Chase was formed it seems likely that the brook
occupied the valley rather than formed it.

On the high point of this route you pass a clump
of young Scots Pines. They are some of hilltop
pines recently planted to replace the Anson's Pines
which commemorated Admiral Anson's voyage round
the world in 1780. A few massive, battered
specimens are still standing near Milford and on
Oat Hill (this one) and Broc Hill (Route (7).

Ansons Pines at Milford

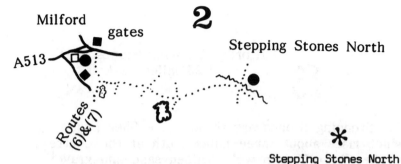

Milford

gates

A513

2

Stepping Stones North

Routes (6)&(7)

✳

**Milford to
Stepping Stones North**

(1) From gates of Shugborough (far side of common from cafes), cross A513 & take rising path.

(2) Go up & between pines, then down to track junction by pool.

(3) Take main track L, cross rise & pass path R by (?dried up) pool, to track R.

(4) Go R up steep gulch to crest. KEEP SAME LINE over summit & past pines R, then DOWN steeply to crosstracks in valley bottom.

(5) Take track ahead appx .3 mile to

Stepping Stones North
●

>> OPTIONS <<
Routes 3(a) or 5(1)

✳

**Stepping Stones North
to Milford**

(a) At stepping stones, put brook behind you flowing L to R

(b) Take track R appx .3 mile to crosstracks. Take steep path ahead up to crest.

(c) KEEP SAME LINE over summit & past pines L, then down, joining steep gulch to meet track.

(d) Go L (pass path L) & over rise to junction of tracks by pool L.

ROUTES 6(3) (Boulderstone) & 7(3) (Oldacre Valley) run L

(e) Go R over crest to common & car park.

Milford
●

>> OPTIONS <<
Routes 1(1), 6(1) or 7(1)

3

Seven Springs - Stepping Stones North
1.25 miles   2 kms

A clear wide path traces the northern edge of the Chase. It is quite level but there are tempting brackeny valleys up between the round sandy hills to the south. Seven Springs is green and gladey with birch, and there are chains of pools at the start of Route 15.

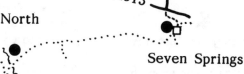

A513

Stepping Stones North

Seven Springs

*

Seven Springs to
Stepping Stones North

(1) Put your back to car park entrance & take track curving R to pole barrier.

(2) Go R appx 1.25 miles to

Stepping Stones North.

●
>> OPTIONS <<
Routes 2(a) or 5(1)

*

Stepping Stones North
to Seven Springs

(a) At stepping stones, put brook behind you flowing R to L

(b) Take track ahead appx 1.25 miles to picnic area/car park.

Seven Springs
●
>> OPTIONS <<
Routes 1(a), 4(1) or 15(1)

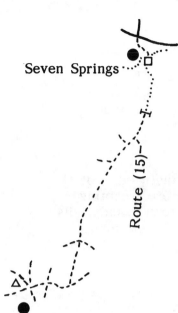

Seven Springs

A513

Route (15)

East Trig Point

4

Seven Springs - East Trig Point
2.2 miles   3.5 kms

A long straight track from the Trent Valley (height 220 feet) up Abrahams's valley to a trig point (650 feet) commanding the northern half of the Chase.

East Trig to Seven Springs

(a) At forest corner track junction, stand in MID JUNCTION with trig point behind.

(b) Take track ahead to cross-tracks, & go ahead down to junction by flag pole.

(c) Go L down valley 1.7 miles to steel barrier on wood edge.

ROUTE 15(4)(Rifle Range Corner)
takes track R over brook
appx 300 yds back

(d) Take track ahead to car park.

Seven Springs
●

>> OPTIONS <<
Routes 1(a), 3(1) or 15(1)

Seven Springs to East Trig

(1) At car park put your back to exit & NB 2 pole barriers ahead.

(2) Pass L barrier on your R & follow path thro wood to join stone track.

(3) Follow appx 1.7 miles to T junction by flag pole.

(4) Go R up to crosstracks & take track ahead to next junction by trig point.

East Trig Point
●

>> OPTIONS <<
Routes 12(a) or 14(a)

(30)

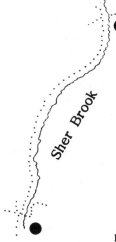

5

Stepping Stones North
-
Stepping Stones South
1.4 miles 2.3 kms

This beautiful path follows the Sher Brook from the gentle birch and oak woodland in the northern Chase, to the more barren heath and pine of the centre. The valley is one of the two main north south incisions in the Chase plateau, the other being Abrahams Valley to the east (Route (4). Oldacre Valley on the western edge is a smaller third which you can explore on Route (7).

Stepping Stones
South

*
Stepping Stones North to
Stepping Stones South

(1) At stepping stones, put stream on your L flowing front to back.

(2) Follow valley track appx 1.4 miles, to junction by post No.7 & stepping stones L.

Stepping Stones South
●
>> OPTIONS <<
Routes 11(a), 12(1) or 13(1)

*
Stepping Stones South to
Stepping Stones North

(a) From stepping stones get on open heath side of valley, on tracks by post No. 7.

(b) Go DOWN valley appx 1.4 miles to next stepping stones.

Stepping Stones North

>> OPTIONS <<
Routes 2(a) or 3(a)

6

Milford - Boulderstone
1.8 miles 3 kms

This route follows a visible remnant of World War I. The deep rising cutting, the curved embankment and the level sections on the crest were the formation of the Tackeroo Railway, a branch built by the Army to supply the training camps. it continues on Routes (10) and (18). Your guess about the meaning of the name will be as good as anybody's.

The Heart of England Way crosses the Chase touching Routes (6), (10), (17), part of (16), (25) and (33). Keep trotting south at Castle Ring and you can walk 100 miles via Lichfield, Meriden, Henley in Arden, Alcester, Bidford on Avon and Chipping Campden to Bourton on the Water in the Cotswolds. (This is a plug because I wrote and published the guide.)

The bulrush pool at the head of the old rail cutting is known as Mere Pool. There have been gravel and sand quarries all over the Chase and this might be one, or it could be due to the peculiar conditions beneath the melting ice sheet, with water rushing in all directions trying to get to the seaside. But my guess is that the navvies took it out in 1914 to build the embankment.

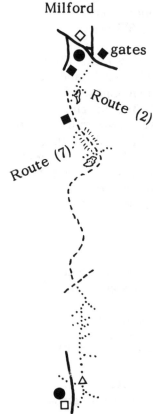

Milford

gates

Route (2)

Route (7)

Boulderstone

6

* Milford to Boulderstone

(1) From gates of Shugborough (far side of common from cafes etc), cross A513 & take rising path opposite to crest.

(2) Go between pines & down, pass pool on your L & join track.

(3) Go down & meet next track. Go L, past house R, to track junction.

(4) Follow deep cutting (parallel path on R is better) to junction by pool R.

(5) Take track ahead curving R & up .6 mile to crosstracks.

(6) Take track opposite appx .3 mile to bend, & fork R.

(7) At next fork go L, down small valley & up, cross a track, then meet track.

(8) Go R & join main level track along ridge, to white trig point R.

Boulderstone
●
>> OPTIONS <<
Routes 8(1), 10(1) or 11(1)

* Boulderstone to Milford

(a) From boulder go to white trig point, then open heath. Go L on level ridge track to next Staffs Way sign.

(b) Track bends R, you go AHEAD, round R bend & take next track L.

(c) Cross a track, go down small valley & up to join track. Go ahead & curve L to tracks & car park.

(d) Take track opposite behind pole barrier appx .6 mile, to track junction & pool L.

(e) Take deep cutting ahead (parallel path on L is better) to junction.

ROUTE 7(4) (Oldacre Valley) runs off here. To use it first face cutting.

(f) Go ahead past house L & take next track R to pool.

ROUTE 2(3) Stepping Stones N runs R. To use it first turn round.

(g) Continue past pines to common & car park.

Milford
●
>> OPTION <<
Routes 1(1), 2(1) or 7(1)

The Tackeroo Railway

In 1915 the Army built a railway to supply the Brocton and Rugeley training camps. Staffs County Council's Great War leaflet (from the Visitor Centre) shows most of the layout but misses two important parts.

The single standard guage track left the Cannock to Rugeley line at Hednesford just south of the Enterprise Centre industrial estate, formerly Cannock No 5 pit. Running uphill beside the road to just south of Nine Gate, it then swung west towards the cemetaries. Originally the line followed the road to the top of Penkridge Bank at Rifle Range Corner, but the gradient was steep and demanded an extra banking engine. The realignment was made after some trucks ran away and were smashed.

A branch and loop ran east to Rugeley Camp around Rifle Range Corner. The main line continued north past the cemetaries where a branch forked off to run on the west side of the Stafford road to Spring Slade. The main line passed east of Spring Slade and over Ansons Bank to the Boulderstone. Here were various loops and sidings. The track ran on (Route (6), past the modern car park on Coppice Hill and down the long bank to Milford. It crossed the Stafford - Rugeley road (A513) and the lane to Tixall to join the London & North Western Railway's main Trent Valley line.

You will find odd platforms and concrete structures close to the line of the old track to help loading and unloading. But there was only one significant piece of engineering, the deep cutting from Milford to Mere Pool, Route (6). Locally this is called the "German Cutting", but there were no Germans about when it was built.

Tackeroo was the name of a row of houses just north from Hednesford at the foot of Brindley Valley, and the start of the camp railway. The inhabitants were said to be surly, short tempered and violent and to have sold watercress and bilberries from the valley. But none of this explains the name, which must be a lot older than the railway. There may be a connection with "truck", or payment of workers in tokens rather than coin, or with "tick". Truck was outlawed in 1835 but decades later some people still called pay day "truckaroo". On Routes (16) and (20) you pass the Forestry Commission's "Tackeroo" Caravan Site. It is close to Rifle Range Corner at the very top of Brindley Valley on the site of one of the Ordnance Stores. With the camp Post Office and two YMCA's nearby, I imagine it was not the ammo dump.

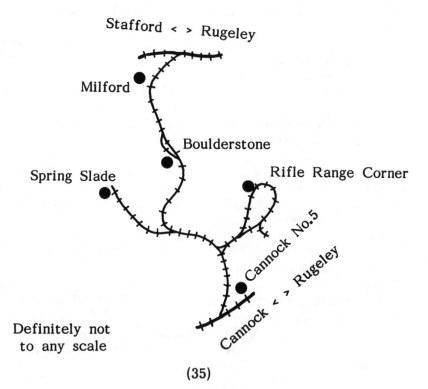

Stafford < > Rugeley

Milford

Boulderstone

Spring Slade

Rifle Range Corner

Cannock No.5

Cannock < > Rugeley

Definitely not
to any scale

(35)

7

Milford - Oldacre Valley
1.8 miles   3 kms

There are small, steep, complicated hills and valleys, a clump of hilltop pines (explanation Route (2), a green causeway between dry pools and the perilous duckboard crossing of a springy, soggy valley bottom.

Milford to Oldacre Valley

(1) From gates of Shugborough (far side of common from cafes etc), cross A513 & take rising path opposite to crest.

(2) Go between pines & down, to pass pool on your L & join track.

(3) Go down & meet next track. Go L, pass house R, to track junction at foot of cutting.

(4) Go to R of cutting & take steep path UP to summit.

(5) Go parallel with new pines on your L plus 30 paces. NB oval path L; go to opposite end & take steep path to valley bottom.

(6) SIGHT valley ahead; go to it & meet cross-track. Go 70 paces up valley & take path R to crest by fence corner.

(7) Take path ahead, pass track R & cross a track, to FENCE CORNER L.

(8) Go on 3 paces & take small path R. Ignore faint path L & go on to meet causeway.

(9) Go R & via paths to drive by white gates. Go L to lane.

(10) Go R a few paces to pole barrier L, & take track behind it. Pass green path R & meet ridge path.

(11) Go L appx 130 paces & take steep path down R. Cross valley & go up to cross-tracks.

(12) Go L up valley appx .3 mile to crosstracks in valley bottom.

Oldacre Valley

●

>> OPTIONS <<
Routes 8(a) or 9(a)

(36)

7

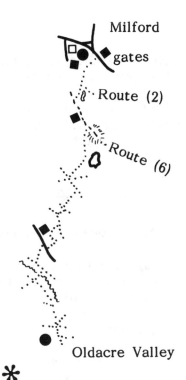

Milford
gates

Route (2)

Route (6)

Oldacre Valley

Oldacre Valley to Milford

(a) At 5 track junction in valley bottom, take path DOWN valley. Pass small path R & at fork go R to crosstracks.

(b) Go R, cross valley & up to track on crest.

(c) Go L appx 130 paces & take path R to lane.

(d) Go R a few paces then L towards white gates. Go R into wood & cross causeway.

(e) Take path L & meet track by fence corner. Go L, cross a track, ignore path L, pass fence corner, & down to valley bottom track.

(f) Go L & meet cross-track. Go ahead ACROSS valley & take steep path under oak to crest.

(g) NB new pines ahead & make for L side. Go parallel with pines on your R, plus 20 paces. Take path ahead down to track junction by deep cutting.

ROUTE 6(4) (Boulderstone)
runs up cutting

(h) Go L past house & take next track R to pool.

ROUTE 2(3) Stepping Stones N
runs off here. To use it
first turn round.

(g) Continue over crests to common & car park.

Milford
●

>> OPTIONS <<
Routes 1(1), 2(1) or 6(1)

8

Boulderstone - Oldacre Valley
500 yds   450 metres

A short link between the summit and this lovely valley using the Staffordshire Way

*

Boulderstone to Oldacre Valley

(1) From boulder, cross road & follow Staffs Way to cross-path.

(2) Go ahead 25 paces to (?bust) signpost. Take path R down to valley bottom. Go R 45 paces to 5 track junction.

Oldacre Valley
●
>> OPTIONS <<
Routes 7(a) or 9(a)

*

Oldacre Valley to Boulderstone

(a) From 5 track junction in valley bottom, go UP valley 45 paces & take path L.

(b) Meet path & go L to road &

Boulderstone
●
>> OPTIONS <<
Route 6(a), 10(1) or 11(1)

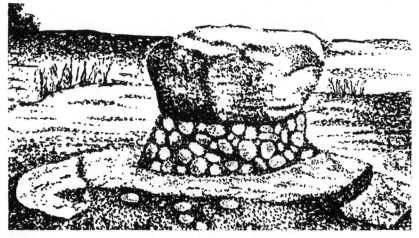

(38)

9

Spring Slade - Oldacre Valley
(via Anson's Bank)
1.5 miles 2.5 kms

Oldacre Valley feels wild and far away. There is birch, heather and bilberry but no main track or forest road. I have seen deer on most visits. The young Scots Pine west of the Stafford - Cannock road are the ultimate contrast. Engineered forest roads swoop in all directions and dark green rides cut the forest into orderly blocks. But I have also seen deer in this place. What do you make of that?

Spring Slade to Oldacre Valley

(1) From cafe by road, take track by cafe appx 350 yds, to gate R & R bend.

(2) Go on appx 110 paces & take path R (becomes track) to meet track.

(3) Go L to cross-track. Take track opposite, then next track R.

(4) Re-enter wood & meet cross-path. Take path opposite to road & car park.

Ansons Bank

(5) In car park face road & go to L side of park. Cross road & take path opposite.

(6) Cross a track & take track ahead to meet track. Go L to green clearing.

(7) Curve round R & resume track. Take next track L to lane.

(8) Go R appx 75 paces & take green track L to meet track.

(9) Take small path opposite to green clearing. Exit via next clearing to valley bottom track.

(10) Go L, ignore 1st cross-track & on to 5 track junction.

Oldacre Valley

●

>> OPTIONS <<
Routes 7(a) or 8(a)

Oldacre Valley

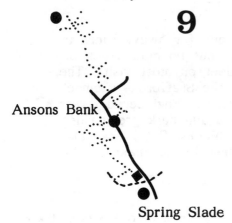

9

Ansons Bank

Spring Slade

Oldacre Valley to Spring Slade

(a) From 5 track junction in valley bottom, go UP valley to next wide cross-track.

(b) SIGHT up valley to green clearing R. Go on appx 110 paces & enter it.

(c) Bear L past central bracken clump & thro green gap to next clearing. Bear L passing central pine on your L, to nearest birch tree.

[Sorry about complications, but we must get you pointing the right way.]

(d) Stand with birch appx 3 yds on your L & pine behind. Go ahead & take small path between 2 birches.

(e) Follow winding path & meet wide green track. Take track opposite to lane.

(f) Go R appx 75 paces & take track L. Round S bend to meet track. Go R to green clearing & CURVE L to take track ahead.

(g) Pass track L & take next track R to road. [CARE]

Ansons Bank

(h) Enter curved car park & take small path at back to cross-path.

(i) Take track ahead to open heath & meet track. Go L to cross-tracks.

(j) Take rising track opposite appx 400 yds, then track R down to valley bottom track.

(k) Go L to road & cafe.

Spring Slade

>> OPTIONS <<
Routes 10(a), 17(1) or 18(a)

10

Boulderstone - Spring Slade
1 mile   1.8 kms

Boulderstone

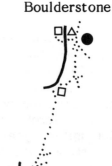

This route follows the Heart of England Way across Anson's Bank. There are fine views of the rolling landscape from near the Boulderstone, and on Anson's Bank is a topograph presented by a firm that makes glue. Near the car park at about midway is a left-over from the First World War. The concrete structure supported a hopper for loading coal wagons on the Tackeroo Railway.

Spring Slade

*

Boulderstone to Spring Slade

(1) From boulder go to trig point, then open heath. Take track R by post No.4.

(2) At post 5 fork R to crosstracks. Go R to car park.

(3) Exit R to road. Go L a few paces & take track L appx .6 mile, over crest, & down to road & cafe.

Spring Slade
●
>> OPTIONS <<
Routes 9(1), 17(1) or 18(a)

*

Spring Slade to Boulderstone

(a) From cafe by road, take sloping path opposite cafe (not Katyn track). Pass 2 tracks R & on over crest appx .6 mile to road & car park.

(b) Enter park. Go to far end & take track L to crosstracks.

(c) Go L to join track at post No.5, then L to trig point L &

Boulderstone
●
>> OPTIONS <<
Routes 6(a), 8(1), or 11(1)

Rocks & Contours

"Geology of Cannock Chase" by Paul Green is comprehensive and fascinating and costs only 50 pence. Get it from the Marquis Drive Visitor Centre. Here is my plain person's homemade account.

Deep beneath the Chase, and the whole region, is a basement layer of ancient rocks formed from the very birth of the earth up to about 350 million years ago. It plays no real part in the structure of the mound we call Cannock Chase. Coal measures (Carboniferous) were formed as the next layer up to 300 million years back, which include coal but also sandstones, ironstones, mudstones and marl clays. These explain why brick making usually goes with coal mining. The measures slope westwards, partly explaining the greater depth of coal on the west side. Littleton Colliery is currently working beneath the Chase, to give some idea of depth, at about 3,000 feet.

From about 230 millions years ago pebble beds were laid down by fast flowing water. (Triassic) They are cemented together into a conglomerate rock and layered with sandstone to a depth of about 480 feet. Most of the pebbles are a grey-purple quartzite which may have come from what is now northern France, but others are sandstones, volcanic rocks, and limestones from south and west England. Most likely, further layers were formed on top of these, but they are not to be found, except for the deposits left by the last ice age.

Between 26,000 and 10,000 years ago a colosal bank of ice covered the Chase and much of Britain to the north. In fact the Chase may have been the tip of a southern salient. At its densest 18,000 years ago, it is usual to say that the ice later "retreated".

But it didn't of course, it melted, and dropped all the rock and soil scooped up over millenia in the great grind south. Melt water formed beneath the glaciers and was forced under great pressure to find a way out. Imagine a sort of insane refrigerated jacuzzi with melt water rushing through ice caves, sometimes uphill, laced with churning pebbles and sand.

The contours you see now are the result of erosion by rain and wind, which has smoothed and sculpted the wild work of the meltwater.

The Chase north of the Rising Brook valley is, more or less, covered with glacial deposits over the Triassic pebble beds. To the south the Carbonif--erous coal measures are near the surface because, at some stage, this part was pushed higher and the Triassic layer eroded away.

On the east and west sides of the Chase are the Rugeley and Bushbury faults. They mark the edges of the Chase and beyond them the ground is the sandstone and marl clay more typical of this part of the Midlands.

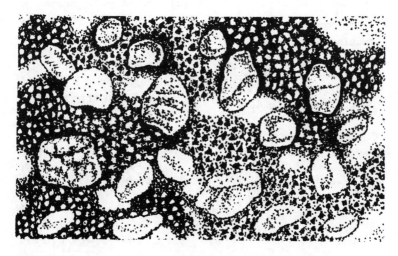

Boulderstone - Stepping Stones South
.7 mile   1.1 kms

From the ice age boulder and the trig point at about 640 feet this short route plunges down to the Sher Brook at 500 feet.

11

The massive granite boulder weighs about 2.5 tonnes and was carried by the ice from Criffel in southern Scotland. The concrete base once supported a monstrous water tank supplying the Army camps.

Boulderstone

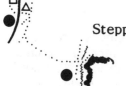

Stepping Stones South

Stepping Stones South
to Boulderstone

*

Boulderstone to
Stepping Stones South

(a) From stepping stones go to open heath side of valley, at track junction by post No.7.

(1) From boulder go to white trig point then open heath. Take track R by post No.4.

(b) Go AHEAD on L of 2 tracks. Curve up R past 2 tracks R, & post No.5, to trig ppint L &

(2) At post No. 5 fork L down to valley bottom track &

Boulderstone
●
>> OPTIONS <<
Routes 6(a), 8(1) or 10(1)

Stepping Stones South
●
>> OPTIONS <<
Routes 5(a), 12(1) or 13(1)

East Trig Point

12

Stepping Stones South
-
East Trig Point
.5 mile .75 kms

A short link up the east side of Sherbrook valley, the counterpart of Route (11).

Stepping Stones South

✳

Stepping Stones South to East Trig Point

(1) From stepping stones take track to trees & meet track.

(2) Go L & with trees on your R. Round R bend & go up to trig point by forest corner.

East Trig Point
●
>> OPTIONS <<
Routes 4(a) or 14(a)

✳

East Trig Point to Stepping Stones South

(a) From trig point by forest corner, take track with open heath on your R.

(b) Go down & round L bend to take next track R.

Stepping Stones South
●
>> OPTIONS <<
Routes 5(a), 11(a) or 13(1)

13

Stepping Stones South

Gospel Place

This is the southern part of the Valley route, Route (5) is to the north. The pines on the east side seem to highten the feeling of sandy wilderness on the open heath to the west. The concrete trough serves as a bridge, but surely you would never build one this way. It may have been a water channel serving some army camp purpose.

You can see how the Sher Brook gradually forms in a damp patch, though there is nothing to see of the brook except the head of a little valley which promises a stream sometime.

Stepping Stones South
to Gospel Place

(1) From stepping stones, get on to open heath side of brook & take track UP valley.

(2) Pass concrete trough over brook L & on to next track junction.

Gospel Place
●
>> OPTIONS <<
Routes 16(a) or 17(a)

Gospel Place to
Stepping Stones South

(a) From track junction in valley 50 yds from forest, edge, take track DOWN valley.

(b) Watch for track junction by post no.7 & stepping stones R.

Stepping Stones South

>> OPTIONS <<
Routes 5(a), 11(a) or 12(1)

Habitats, Plants & Creatures

This is not a book on the natural history of Cannock Chase and I will not list all the rare and curious plants and creatures. Their names mean nothing to most readers, but they may be interested to see the different types of habitat on the Chase and how they support different species. There is a separate section on the deer.

The Chase is mainly covered by loose, free draining sandy gravel, and plant nutrients tend to be washed out, making it dry and poor. This is obvious on the open heath where there are heathers and bracken, bilberry and its relations the cowberry and crowberry. The Cannock Chase berry is a unique local hybrid. There are tough grasses such as wavy hair grass, bents, fescues and matt grass. Beside the heathland tracks in sunny places are heath bedstraw, tormentil, eyebright, trefoils and speedwell. Birds include the uncommon hen harrier and great grey shrike, a few whinchat and linnets, with more ordinary meadow pipits and skylarks.

The Chase's most important breeding bird is the nightjar, which nests on open heath with a scatter of birch and pine and where conifers have been felled. Although declining, there are more on the Chase than anywhere else in the Midlands. The Forestry Commission have cut a lot of timber in the last few years and we can be hopeful.

The dry heathy character of the open Chase is greatly modified in places to support very different plants and creatures. On Brocton Hill and Brindley Heath because of disturbance by the Great War and RAF camps, there is a scrubby mixture of hawthorn, gorse, brambles, rosebay and thistles.

The decidous woodland of birch, oak and rowan near Seven Springs and Sycamore Hill make a more fertile and sheltered environment. Brocton Coppice is an ancient sessile oakwood with some trees over 350 years old. There is alder woodland along the Sher Brook, Shropshire Brook, and Stoney Brook. All the woods have hawthorne, elder, crab apple and holly. Beech is most often a planted screen around conifer plantations. The trees shelter a rich and complex community of insects and birds such as the pied flycatcher, redstart and wood warbler. There are also fungii with strange names such as sickener, funnel chartarelle and the highy toxic fly agaric.

Birds in the mixed woodlands include the expected blackbirds, thrushes, magpies, tits, jays and woodpeckers, Look out for the long tailed tit which builds a neat hanging nest.

The damp places form another type of habitat. You will find them in the valleys of the brooks, the moist bottoms of streamless valleys and slighly boggy places in the open, such as near the military cemetries. Peat has developed in the Sherbrook and Oldacre Valleys. So we can add to the Chase flora marsh plants like crossleaved heath, bog asphodel, sundews and marsh violet. In Sherbrook Valley a big tussock sedge grows close to the water. Birds in this habitat are siskins, redpolls and the tits

The poorest habitat on the chase is in the conifer plantations. When the pines are young they are grown close packed to get rid of side branches and grow knot free timber, so they exclude light. The needles are slow to break down and when they do, form an acid matt, and so the forest floor is quite sterile. But the pines do attract some birds, crossbills, coal tits, goldcrests, tawney and long eared owls and an uncommon bird of prey, the hobby.

(48)

14

Rifle Range Corner - East Trig Point
1 mile   1.6 kms

This route belongs to the blackly forested, southern part of the Chase. But beech trees on the edges of paths prettily soften the impact, if they do nothing much for the bare interior.

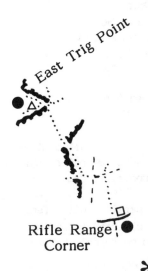

East Trig Point

Rifle Range Corner

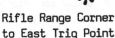

*

Rifle Range Corner
to East Trig Point

(1) In car park, face information board. Take path in L corner to T junction at stone track.

(2) Go L, cross track, pass gate R & on to track junction.

(3) Go R & thro forest to track junction on forest corner by trig point.

East Trig Point
●
>> OPTIONS <<
Routes 4(a) or 12(a)

East Trig Point
to Rifle Range Corner

(a) At forest corner track junction, stand in MID JUNCTION with trig point on your R & take track ahead,

(b) Follow to T junction with pole barrier R & go L. Pass gate L & cross track.

(c) Go on appx 100 yds & take path R by power pole.

ROUTE 15(b) (Seven Springs) follows path opposite

(d) Follow path to car park near
Rifle Range Corner
●
>> OPTIONS <<
Routes 15(a), 16(1) or 20(1)

Seven Springs - Rifle Range Corner
3 miles   5 kms

Between the Trent Valley at 220 feet and Penkridge Bank at 620, there is a chain of clear pools at Seven Springs, the straight and ancient Sow or South Street from Colwich to Cannock and a secretive valley of heather and bilberry.

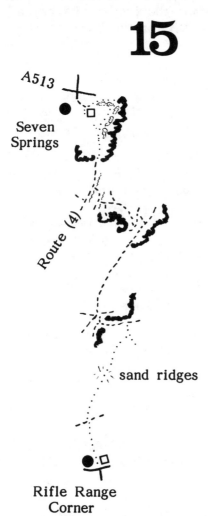

15

A513

Seven
Springs

Route (4)

sand ridges

Rifle Range
Corner

* Seven Springs to
Rifle Range Corner

(1) Leave car park past pool by entrance. Follow paths thro wood to boundary fence.

(2) Go R, parallel with fence (path gets clearer) & join path from R. Go on to pole barrier.

(3) Go ahead on stone track appx 300 yds & take track L.

(4) Round R bend & on to take next bend L over brook.

(5) Take track ahead, pass flagpole & track R, past track L, to T junction near crest.

(6) Go L to next junction & R to wide main ridge track.

(7) Go R appx .6 mile to R bend with tracks R & L & EARTH MOUND across track L.

(8) Take earth mound track a few paces to junction. Go L to track junction by fence corner.

(9) Take track R DOWN to valley bottom track.

(10) Go R up valley bottom track appx 400 yds to sharp L bend.

(11) Bear R on small path over sand ridges, & on up valley bottom path.

15

(12) Near top ignore small paths R & curve L to meet stone track.

ROUTE 14(2) (East Trig Point) runs R. "Go R ..."

(13) Take path opposite to car park near

Rifle Range Corner

●

>> OPTIONS <<

Routes 14(1), 16(1) or 20(1)

*

Rifle Range Corner
to Seven Springs

(a) In car park, face information board. Take path at L corner to its end at stone track.

(b) Take small path opposite, curving R down VALLEY BOTTOM to sand ridges.

(c) Cross ridges & bear R to rejoin valley bottom track. [Track may be interrupted by wide disturbed strip.] Go appx 400 yds & meet cross-path just before marsh in old quarry.

(d) Take path L up to track junction by fence corner.

(e) Go L to sharp L bend. Take short track R past earth mound to main track.

(f) Go ahead appx .6 mile, past 1st conservation sign to 2nd.

(g) Take track opposite sign to next junction. Go L & take next track R. Go down, past tracks R & L to cross brook.

(h) Go R to cross brook & join valley track.

ROUTE 4(3) (East Trig Point) runs L

(i) Go R, pass pole barrier into wood & take 1st path R.

(j) Go with brook on your R as far as possible, then L on paths to car park.

Seven Springs

●

>> OPTIONS <<

Routes 1(a), 3(1) or 4(1)

(51)

Rifle Range Corner - Gospel Place
1 mile   1.6 kms

The central Chase is less hilly than the north or south and this route falls only about 60 feet to the head of Sher Brook Valley. The rifle ranges were part of the army camps. One to the north-east of the Chase is still in use. There are big disused buts near the East Trig Point and you cross a small one on Route (15).

16

Rifle Range Corner

Gospel Place

Route (20)

*

Rifle Range Corner
to Gospel Place

(1) From car park exit to road. Take drive opposite appx 160 yds & take 1st of 2 tracks R.

(2) Go to road bend, cross & take L of 2 tracks.

(3) Follow into & thro trees to open heath. Go on 50 yds to crosstracks in valley bottom.

Gospel Place
●
>> OPTIONS <<
Routes 13(a) or 17(a)

*

Gospel Place
to Rifle Range Corner

(a) From crosstracks in valley, take track into forest appx .75 mile to road bend.

(b) Cross road & take woodland path to meet drive.

ROUTE 20(2) (Fairoak)
runs R

(c) Go L & cross road to car park.

Rifle Range Corner
●
>> OPTIONS <<
Routes 14(1), 15(a) or 20(1)

Gospel Place is a remote sandy place at the head of Sherbrook Valley, with open heath on the west side and forest to the east. The Brook is the boundary between two parishes, and the name has something to do with beating the bounds on Rogation Day. This explanation seems to fall short of the full story, whatever it is. But I can imagine a bearded man in robe and sandals preaching to a multitude.

This is one of the best open heath walks, on a wide pebbly track with wide views. With the Military Cemetaries to the north this is a fitting place for the Katyn Memorial.

Spring Slade - Gospel Place
.6 mile   1 km

Spring Slade

17

Gospel Place

Gospel Place
to Spring Slade

✳

Spring Slade to
Gospel Place

(a) From crosstracks in valley, take track away from forest appx .6 mile to road & cafe.

(1) From cafe on road, take Katyn Memorial track appx .6 mile, to crosstracks in valley 50 yds before forest.

Spring Slade
●
>> OPTIONS <<
Routes 9(1), 10(a) or 18(a)

Gospel Place
●
>> OPTIONS <<
Routes 13(a) or 16(a)

18

Nine Gate - Spring Slade
2.5 miles   4 kms

Place names on the Chase can often be connected with one of the events described in this book. Nine Gate was a gate to RAF Hednesford, the World War II airforce training camp which stood on the site of the Visitor Centre, and surrounding acres.

This route crosses Brindley Heath, one of the main Great War camp sites, and passes the Military Cemetaries. There are pine forest tracks and breezy open heath, which is being stealthily colonized by birch.

Nine Gate to Spring Slade

(1) From car park with twin birches, take drive down to road.

(2) Go L appx 150 yds & take 1st track R.

(3) Follow appx 1 mile to road.

(4) Go R on verge appx 200 yds. [GREAT CARE] Take track opposite to road.

(5) [CARE] Take path opposite to meet path on bend. Go L to track at cemetery corner.

(6) Cross & take path with cemetary fence on your L. At next fence corner, cross track & follow path onto open heath.

(7) Pass 2 paths L & head for birch clump ahead. Path bends R, you go on to car park.

(8) Turn R. Exit via pole barrier AHEAD & follow path to start of birch strip.

(9) Jink R to parallel path & continue down to track. Go L to road & cafe at

Spring Slade
●
>> OPTIONS <<
Routes 9(1), 10(a) or 17(a)

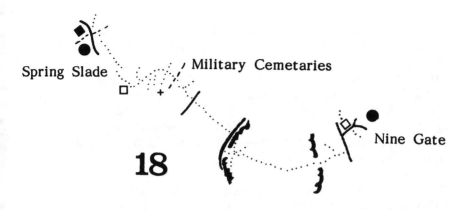

Spring Slade   Military Cemetaries

Nine Gate

18

*

Spring Slade to Nine Gate

(a) From cafe on road take Katyn Memorial track a few paces, then 1st path R.

(b) Follow up to open heath. At END of birch strip R, jink R to parallel path. Keep same line to car park.

(c) Go to central twin birches. Turn L & take small path, bearing R along edge of heath.

(d) Pass 2 paths R & cross wide track, then with cemetary R, to track on next cemetery corner.

(e) Bear a little R across track & take path up edge of pines 80 paces, to path bend.

(f) Take path R to road. [GREAT CARE] Take track opposite to road.

(g) Cross & go R on verge appx 200 yds. Take track L.

(h) At 5 tracks junction, go ahead (ie 3rd from L), appx 1 mile to road.

(i) Go L appx 150 yds & take drive R to small car park L with twin birches.

Nine Gate
●
>> OPTIONS <<
Routes 19(1), 22(1) or 23(1)

The Military Cemetries

At Broadhurst Green on the Cannock - Stafford road
there are now Commonwealth and German cemetaries.
From 1916 a single burial ground held the victims
of illness and accidents in the camps. Many had
died in the deadly Spannish Influenza epidemic of
1918, relatively few were war casualties. The
graves are mainly those of New Zealanders and
Germans, since most of the British could be takem
home for burial.

In 1960 it was decided to bury here all Germans
who had died in Britain in both wars, and German
students prepared a new plot. But the Great War
dead were left where they lay, British, New
Zealanders and Germans together.

In 1973 the custom of an annual service on ANZAC
Day (25th April) was revived. It is now organised
by the Royal British Legion and people come from
all over Britain and the world.

About half a mile north at Spring Slade is a newer,
more shocking, memorial with no graves. On a slate
pediment is a stone inscribed,

> "In memorial to the 14,000 members of the
> Polish armed forces and professional classes
> who were executed in the Katyn Forest,
> nineteen hundred and fourty (1940)".

This mass murder was blamed blamed on the Nazis for
some fifty years, but glasnost produced conclusive
evidence that it was committed by Soviet forces.

The clean windy Chase with its heath and pine
forests, its tangled, sad history and military
past seems a fitting place to remember.

Fairoak

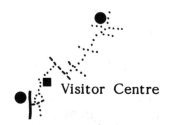

Visitor Centre

Nine Gate

19

Nine Gate - Fairoak
(via Visitor Centre)
1 mile 1.5 kms

This walk samples a little of wild heath and some of the managed forest. It rises about 70 feet between the valley of the Stoney Brook and the Visitor Centre.

Fairoak to Nine Gate

*

Nine Gate to Fairoak

(1) In car park with twin birches, put your back to drive & find small path.

(2) Go up to crest & round R bend to meet path. Go L, ignore small paths L, & curve R past blue/red post to car park.

Marquis Drive Visitor Centre

(3) From car park go to Centre & pass it on your R, then bear R to orange finger post.

(4) Follow grass strip with fence on your R to drive. Go R & take 1st forest track L.

(5) Follow down to crosstracks at valley bottom.

(a) From crosstracks at valley bottom, put POST NO.3 ON YOUR R & take track with POWER LINES up to drive.

(b) Go R with fence on your L. Take 1st gap L & head for

Marquis Drive Visitor Centre

(c) From centre go to car park. Bear L thro centre of line of wood posts & take path.

(d) Follow past blue/red post, ignore 2 small paths R & at L bend, take path R.

(e) Follow round L bend & down to car park.

Fairoak

●

>> OPTIONS <<
Routes 20(a) or 21(1)

Nine Gate

●

>> OPTIONS <<
Routes 18(1), 22(1) or 23(1)

War and the Chase

Between the autumn of 1914 and mid 1915 the Army organised a railway, three miles of road, ten miles of sewerage and water pipes, electricity lines, and wooden huts for two infantry divisions with their artillery. Planned for about 23,000 men and 5,500 horses, there were stores, cookhouses, messrooms, stables, canteens, guardrooms and indoor ranges. Later came a post office, cinema, hospital, banks and a W H Smiths.

"A Town for Four Winters" by CJ & GP Whitehouse describes the Great War Army camps. "Kitbag Hill" by CJ Whitehouse is the story of RAF Hednesford from 1938. Both books are admirably researched and illustrated with maps and photos, and are published by Messrs Whitehouse. Staffs County Council also publish a handy leaflet with a big sketch map on the Chase in the Great War.

Get these definitive histories from the Visitor Centre if you want to persue the subject; here I will just outline some of the main features.

There were two camps. Brocton sat along the ridge between Oldacre Valley and Sherbrook, where the Boulderstone stands, with a detached portion on Ansons Bank. Rugeley Camp was around what we now call Rifle Range Corner and the hospital was alone on Brindley Heath.

The camps gave basic infantry training (scouting, PT, signalling, shooting) but there never were two complete divisions there as planned. It housed reserve and training units, and sometimes active units in transit. The book lists battalions from many regiments.

The New Zealand Rifle Brigade ("The Dinks") spent
time on the Chase, and built a concrete scale model
of the Messines Ridges, site of a sucessfull allied
attack in 1917. Gorse covered remains lie a few
yards west of Route (6), where the railway track
reached the start of the slope down to Milford.

German prisoners of war were installed as the war
drew on, guarded with the usual dismal apparatus of
wire and watch towers manned by wounded British
soldiers unfit for combat. Later the POWs were sent
out to work on local farms.

The Chase was raw and treeless in 1915 as it had
been for two centuries. An infantryman wrote home
"This is a horrible place on top of a hill ... The
cold is dreadful and always a wind blowing and dust
flying". Bleak photographs show ranks of wood and
tin huts, telegraph wires and grey flatness.

RAF Hednesford was not built on the site of the
Great War camps, they had gone twenty years before,
sewers choked, hut bases and roads under conifers.
In 1938 it was cheaper to build a new camp on the
plateau above Moors Gorse, with extra housing for
instructors at Pye Green and Penkridge Bank. There
were to be 800 staff, and up to 4,000 trainees.

Arrivals came by rail from Rugeley or Hednesford to
Moors Gorse, where a platform was called Brindley
Halt. Then they hauled their kit up Marquis Drive
to the camp, so it became Kitbag Hill.

The camp was officially "No 6 School of Technical
Training", running courses for flight mechanics and
riggers. Some 81,000 men passed through and under a
different title it continued until December 1956.
Ten days later the huts were in use as an emergency
home for 1,200 Hungarian refugees.

The camps are now lumps of lost concrete, ditches and ramps, odd patches of cracked and mossy tarmac, ridges of sand yielding copper bullet cases with splatters of lead, and ghostly floorplans of buildings in the rosebay.

To see what there is, carry the Great War leaflet as you walk these Routes:

Routes (6), (10) and (18) more or less follow the camp railway.

Route (6), (7) and (9) pass through Brocton Camp.

Routes (14), (16) and (20) are in the area of Rugeley Camp.

Routes (19), (22) and (23) go through the RAF camp, part of which is now the Visitor Centre.

Concrete trough over the Sher Brook between Rugeley and Brocton Camps. Used for what?

20

Rifle Range
Corner

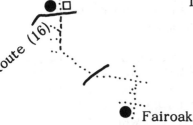

Route (16)

Fairoak

Rifle Range Corner - Fairoak
1 mile 1.6 miles

Scenically this is not the most interesting route in the network, but OK if you like caravan sites, and you can ponder about why it is called Tackeroo. Theories are offered on other pages.

✳

Rifle Range Corner to Fairoak

(1) From car park, exit to road & take track opposite.

(2) Pass caravan site & round L bend to road.

(3) [CARE] Take track opposite to crosstracks by houses.

(4) Go R, pass garage on your L to fork. Go L down to crosstracks at valley bottom.

Fairoak
●
>> OPTIONS <<
Routes 19(a) or 21(1)

✳

Fairoak to Rifle Range Corner

(a) From crosstracks in valley, put post No 3 on your L & take steep track with POWER LINES to join track.

(b) Go ahead & pass house to crosstracks. Go L to road.

(c) [CARE] Take track opposite, round R bend & pass caravan site L.

ROUTE 16(2) (Gospel Place follows 2nd track L after site

(d) Go ahead & cross road to car park.

Rifle Range Corner
●
>> OPTIONS <<
Routes14(1), 15(a) or 16(1)

21

Fairoak - Stoneybrook
.6 miles   1 km

A chain of calm pools has been formed by dams across the Stoney Brook. For some reason those at the western end are called Fairoak Pools and the rest, Stoneybrook Pools. Whether or not the anglers catch anything, this deep sandy valley in the pines is as fine a place to sit and muse as any on the Chase.

Like the Sher Brook which features on other routes, the Old Brook down Abraham's Valley (Route (4), and the Rising Brook along the A460 Rugely-Cannock road, the Stoney Brook flows towards the Trent which is some 200 feet lower.

Fairoak   Stoneybrook

Stoneybrook to Fairoak

(a) At stepping stones, stand with stream behind you flowing L to R.

(b) Go L & follow valley track. Pass fork R & pools L to crosstracks by post No.3.

*

Fairoak to Stoneybrook

(1) At crosstracks by post No.3, go DOWN valley past all pools to crosstrack, then R to stepping stones.

Stoneybrook
●
>> OPTIONS <<
Routes 26(a) & 27(1)

Fairoak
●
>> OPTIONS <<
Routes 19(a) & 20(a)

22

Nine Gate - Moors Gorse
1.4 miles   2.3 kms

Mossy tarmac tracks through silver birch and upland meadows, the corpse of RAF Hednesford is one of the most glowingly beautiful parts of the Chase. Very odd.

Nine Gate

Moors Gorse

A460

*

Nine Gate to Moors Gorse

(1) From car park with twin birches, take drive UP to T junction.

(2) Go R in straight line .5 mile to sharp L bend.

(3) Go L a pace, take track R appx 50 yds, then 1st path L.

(4) Follow to bottom & meet track. Go R, cross railway & A460 [GREAT CARE] to car park.

Moors Gorse
●

>> OPTIONS <<
Routes 24(a) & 25(1)

*

Moors Gorse to Nine Gate

(a) From car park cross A460 [GREAT CARE] & take track opposite. Cross railway & on appx 200yds past house R, to 1st path L.

(b) Take path L up to crest, crossing a path, to meet curving path.

(c) Go R to hard track. Go L a few paces & round R bend, then straight ahead appx .5 mile to end of track & STEEP drive L.

(d) Go L down to car park R with twin birches.

Nine Gate
●

>> OPTIONS <<
Routes 19(1), 18(1) & 23(1)

Nine Gate - Golf Club
(via Cannock No.5)
3 miles 5 kms

A walk beside a golf course sounds reasonable, but do not be put off by the skeleton of the RAF camp and reclaimed mine. The mine is a recent job and looks it, but will soon be as attractive and leafy as the other two. The Chase is asserting itself. Cannock No.5 was the name of the mine, but it is now a small industrial estate with car park.

23

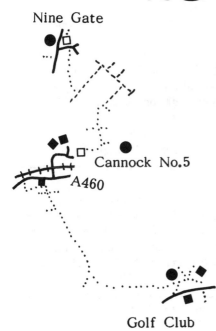

Nine Gate

Cannock No.5

A460

Golf Club

Nine Gate to Golf Club

(1) From car park with twin birches, take drive up a FEW paces to find post No.9 on R.

(2) Take path by post appx .3 mile to meet hard track.

(3) Go L, pass post No.6 to junction by No.5. Go R, pass 2 tracks L & take next track R.

(4) Pass stub track L to new surface & curve L. Pass track R & 1st gate L. Pass 2nd gate L, & curve R to car park.

Cannock No.5

(5) Leave car park via drive. At junction, go down L to A460.

(6) Go R appx 400 yds past works L. [GREAT CARE] Take gate/gap in wall L.

(7) Go with fence on your L to corner, then L to "private" sign.

(8) Go R between white posts & on track appx 150 yds to R bend

(9) Go L thro soil heaps, then concrete blocks, & join rising track with golf course L.

(10) Follow track with course on your L appx 1.25 mile, to crosstracks by golf waiting area.

Golf Club
●
>> OPTIONS <<
Routes 24(b) & 33(n)

23

*

Golf Course to Nine Gate

(a) At golf club waiting area, stand at crosstracks with clubhouse behind & take track with course on your R.

(b) Follow appx 1.25 miles to track end at pole barrier.

(c) Take path skirting green & rejoin track. Pass thro concrete blocks & soil heaps, to track bend.

(d) Go R, cross track via white posts to fence. Go L along it to corner, then R to A460.

(e) [GREAT CARE] Cross & go R. Take drive R (Enterprise Thingy), pass pit wheel, take next drive R. Pass buildings & bend L into car park.

Cannock No.5

(f) Leave car park on corner path by red sign. Pass 1st gate R & 2nd, & curve R. Pass stub track R to T junction.

(g) Go L, pass 2 tracks R to post No.5 & junction. Go L past post No.6 & on 80 pace, to new surface & path R.

(h) Go R appx .3 mile to track & go L a few paces to car park.

Nine Gate
●
>> OPTIONS <<
Routes 18(1), 19(1) & 22(1)

24

Golf Club - Moors Gorse
1.25 miles   2 kms

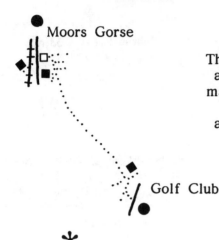

Moors Gorse

Golf Club

A direct and rather barren route through the conifers. There are no ponds, no brooks, and not much grass. It might make it marginally less boring if I tell you that it runs along a slight ridge. OK - so it's still boring.

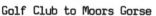

Golf Club to Moors Gorse

(1) At crosstracks by golf waiting area, take track to PASS CLUBHOUSE ON YOUR R.

(2) Follow appx 1 mile (tracks join from R & L). Pass house on your L & on to meet track.

(3) Go L to car park by A460.

Moors Gorse
●
>> OPTIONS <<
Routes 22(a) & 25(1)

Moors Gorse to Golf Club

(a) From car park leave A460 behind & take track past water works R to 1st fork.

(b) Go R, at 2nd fork go R. At 3rd NB 4 paths. Take 2nd from L

(c) Follow appx 1 mile to golf waiting area at crosstracks.

Golf Club
●
>> OPTIONS <<
Routes 23(a) & 34(a)

25

Moors Gorse - Lower Cliff
.6 mile   1 km

Moors Gorse

A460

Lower Cliff

A deep sandy valley and a fine pool. This track is part of Marquis Drive, built by the Marquis of Anglesey to link his home at Beaudesert with the hunting in Sherbrook Valley.

*

Moors Gorse to Lower Cliff

(1) From car park, leave A460 behind & take valley track appx .6 mile to R fork by pool.

Lower Cliff
●
>> OPTIONS <<
Routes 26(1), 28(1) & 35(a)

Lower Cliff to Moors Gorse

(a) At track junction by pool, put your back to minor track (so pool is on R). Go L DOWN valley appx .6 mile to car park & A460.

Moors Gorse

>> OPTIONS <<
Routes 22(a) & 24(a)

Lower Cliff - Stoneybrook
1.7 miles   2.8 kms

This route crosses the deep valley between Cannock
and Rugeley which splits the Chase in two. In fact
after the plateau of the Chase itself, this is by
far its most significant physical feature. Near
Lower Cliff I have devised a curious detour to use
an attractive little back path to pass two noble
beech trees. This is shared by Route (28)

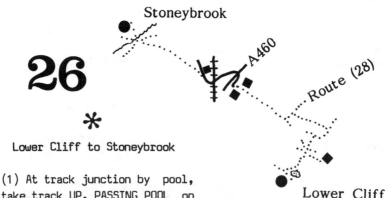

Lower Cliff to Stoneybrook

(1) At track junction by pool,
take track UP, PASSING POOL on
YOUR R.

(2) Go appx 200yds & find mark
post L (150 yds before house).

(3) Take path L by post, cross
a track & take GRASS TRACK
AHEAD, down to meet track.

(4) Go R, curve L & take next
track L (becomes path), to meet
track.

(5) Go L to main track & R down
valley, appx .6 mile to end.

(6) Go R up to A460 & cross.
[CARE] Take lane opposite under
railway & on to just   past
houses R. Take track opposite.

(7) Follow appx .5 mile to
stream & stepping stones at

Stoneybrook

>> OPTIONS <<
Routes 21(a) & 27(1)

(68)

26

*

Stoneybrook to Lower Cliff

(a)   At stepping stones, put stream behind you & flowing R to L.

(b) Go ahead on main track .5 mile to road.

(c) Go R to A460 & cross. [GREAT CARE] Take slip road down & follow valley track appx 25 mile to 1st track L.

ROUTE 28 (India Hills) runs L, para (5) sentence 2. "Follow .... "

(d) Take track L a few paces, then go R on small path (parallel with main valley track) to meet track.

(e) Go R & curve R to big beech trees L by wooden post.

(f) Take grass track L, cross a track & on via small path to bend of main track by mark post

(g) Go R to meet track L by pool.

Lower Cliff
●
>> OPTIONS <<
Routes 25(a), 28(1) & 35(a)

(69)

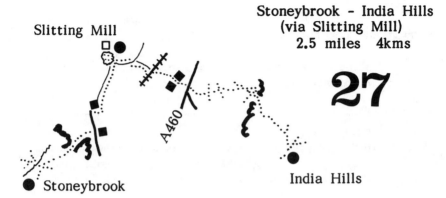

Slitting Mill

27

Stoneybrook

India Hills

Near Stoneybrook there are wide tracks through the conifers. At the other end are more woods but very steep and with a mix of beech and oak. In between are field paths, some rootling pigs and a visit to the fine pool at Slitting Mill.

Stoneybrook to India Hills
(via Slitting Mill)

(1) At stepping stones stand with brook behind & flowing R to L. Go ahead a few paces & take track L.

(2) Follow to road. Go L appx 200 yds. Take track R just before houses to field.

(3) Go L up field edge & cross bridge to pool. Go on to pool corner.

(4) At pool corner put your back to pool & take path DOWN to field.

(5) Go with hedge on your R to field corner by iron fence, then R thro gap.

(6) Cross grass & go L, cross bridge. Follow field edge & under railway.

(7) Follow track up to & thro farm to A460. [GREAT CARE]

(8) Cross & enter hedge gap opposite. NB ahead end of hedge midfield. Take paths ahead or R to it.

Slitting Mill

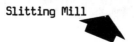

(9) Go with hedge on your L & keep same line. Cross tracks (1) & (2) to where path joins from L.

(10) Count 65 paces & take small path R by fence, thro thicket, to track T junction.

(11) Take track ahead appx .3 mile, up to meet track & power lines.

(12) Go up R to track junction on crest.

India Hills
●
>> OPTIONS <<
Routes 28(a), 29(a) or 30(a)

27

India Hills to Stoneybrook
(via Slitting Mill)

(a) At 5 ways junction under 2 sets of power lines, take wide track DOWN with ONE set of lines on your L.

(b) Take 1st track L, appx .3 mile to T junction of tracks.

(c) Take small path opposite THRO THICKET to track. Go L, pass R fork, & keep same line over 1st track to 2nd.

(d) Go ahead with hedge on your R to its end, then on to A460.

(e) [GREAT CARE] Enter farm opposite, go thro yard, down track & under railway.

(f) Go L into next field then R on field edge to cross bridge.

(g) Go L 20 paces, then R into field corner. Go L on field edge & up to pool.

Slitting Mill

(h) At pool corner, take level path with pool on your R. Cross bridge & follow field edge to stone post & gate R.

(i) Go R to road. Go L appx 200 yds & take track R opposite house "Windward".

(j) Follow appx .3 mile to T junction of tracks. Go down R to brook.

Stoneybrook
●
>> OPTIONS <<
Routes 21(a) & 26(a)

Iron Wood & Coal

Records of 1231 mention iron smelting, casting and forging around Rugeley. By 1300 there was an iron mine and in 1472 a forge was set up at Hednesford.

Staffordshire County Council publish a leaflet on charcoal and iron production which you can get from Marquis Drive Visitor Centre. Briefly, it explains the old method of smelting as heating the ore in an open hearth with charcoal, producing an impure spongy blob of iron. This was reheated and consolidated by hammering. It produced indifferent iron and was time consuming, but needed no capital. The indirect or furnace method was used elsewhere by 1550, and was brought to the Chase by Lord Paget in 1561. Ore, charcoal and limestone were fed into a twenty foot high brick tower. Bellows blew air into the base raising the temperature to 1400 degrees, and molten iron flowed out of the base.

William Paget was a close advisor of Henry VIII and in 1546 had bought most of the Chase from the Crown. Local ironstone, limestone and timber for charcoal, with streams such as the Rising Brook to power bellows, made the Chase an ideal place for an iron works. Getting a licence to fell in 1560, Paget cut acres of oakwoods. But they were Roman Catholics, and under a Protestant Queen collided with the authorities, so Paget was imprisoned in 1580. In 1583 he was implicated in the Throckmorton Plot to kill Elizabeth I and put Mary back on the throne and fled the country. The Crown seized his land but in 1589 leased it for a low rent to Fulke Greville, a rascally favourite of Elizabeth I.

Greville savaged the Chase. On the waste that was left there was no fire wood, no building timber and no more for charcoal. In the teeth of bitter criticism and a national inquiry, Greville went on felling until the end of his lease.

Coal mining was recorded at Beaudesert in 1298, 1367, 1440 and 1497. There were "bell pits" for shallow seams and their remains can be seen at Beaudesert and Brindley Heath. Open cast methods were used in some places, and in others drifts, in which tunnels were driven into a hillside.

Coke smelting replaced charcoal by 1757, but richer easier seams lay to the south and Chase coal could not complete. Rolling and slitting of iron bars to make nails, chains and other hardware had been carried on since 1623, and this now became the main work of the area until the mid 1800's. This explains the big square pool, two waterfalls and the name of the village of Slitting Mill.

From about 1850 deep mines were sunk round the Chase. There are faults in the coal measures on both sides, throwing coal to 1700 feet to the west and 200 feet in the east. The nearest pits were at Chasetown, Hednesford, Cannock, Norton Canes and near Rugeley. They have all closed except the Littleton at Huntington north of Cannock, and that is threatened (Jan 1993). Mines tunnel for miles and all over the Chase you will see gloomy little yellow notices. British Coal are warning you that the ground may sink a little under your feet. The only mining is now from Littleton at a depth of 3000 feet which will have few effects at the surface. Old workings may cause some movement.

Quarrying for gravel, sand and building stone has been carried on for centuries on the Chase. Worked out pits can be found here and there but their scale was modest. Not modest at all are the workings at Bevins Birches and Pottal Pool.

Lower Cliff - India Hills (via Stile Cop)
1.8 miles 3 kms

This route rises 200 feet in a quarter of a mile
yet most of it is level, along the ridge from
Stile Cop. From this high point you can see miles
of small hills and the cooling towers of Rugeley
power station, if you like that sort of thing.
Erotically curved, they have the grace of all well
engineered objects, like electricity pylons. They
too are always in the wrong place.

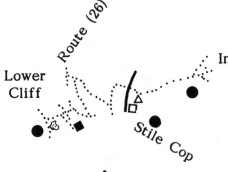

28

Route (26)

Lower
Cliff

India Hills

Stile Cop

*

Lower Cliff to India Hills
(via Stile Cop)

(1) At T junction of tracks by
pool, put your back to minor
track & go up R.

(2) Go appx 200yds & find mark
post L (150 yds before house).

(3) Take path L by post, cross
a track & take grass track
ahead, down to meet track.

(4) Go R & take next track L
(becomes path), to meet track.

(5) Go R. Follow steep track to
meet level track. Go L, round
R bend & on to road. [CARE]

(6) Take path opposite, bear
round R & up to concrete trig
point at
            Stile Cop.

(7) At trig point face cooling
towers. Take any of 3 paths
ahead along ridge.

(8) Paths part & rejoin to
follow ridge. Go on appx 500
yds to 5 track junction beneath
2 sets of power lines.

India Hills
●

>> OPTIONS <<
Routes 27(a), 29(a) & 30(a)

(74)

✱ 28

India Hills to Lower Cliff
(via Stile Cop)

(a) At 5 track junction under power lines, stand with steep track down on your R. Take track ahead along ridge.

(b) Stay on RIDGE (follow any path - they rejoin), heading for summit & trig point at

Stile Cop.

(c) At trig point, put your back to cooling towers & take path down R. Bear L round to road.

(d) Take track opposite. Round L bend & on appx 150 yds to take steep track down R.

(e) Follow to bottom & small path L, (stone track is ahead).

ROUTE 26 (Stoneybrook) runs R down valley (para 4)

(f) Take small path L to meet track.

(g) Go R & curve R to big beech trees L by wooden post.

(h) Take grass track L, cross a track & on via small path to bend of track by mark post.

(i) Go R to meet track L by pool.

Lower Cliff
●
>> OPTIONS <<
Routes 25(a), 26(1) & 35(a)

The Deer

The Chase has foxes, badgers, rabbits, stoats and
weasels, voles, shrews and woodmice. There are
thousands of grey squirrels, a few red squirrels
in the conifers, many adders and a few slow worms,
grass snakes and lizards. But what most visitors
watch for are the deer.

Marquis Drive Visitor Centre has an exhibition on
all aspects of the Chase, but especially the deer.
Here you can learn to recognise them and make your
own slot (hoof) marks in a sand pit. Look out for
the bracket like marks - () - in any soft ground.

There are red, fallow and muntjac species. The
traffic sign shows most people's idea of the
creatures, a red stag with many pointed antlers.
The designer should have taken advice because on
the Chase, as in most of England and Wales, there
are few red but many fallow.

Fallow deer roam wild over the whole Chase. There
may be 600 and numbers have to be kept in check or
they can outrun their food supply. The Foresty
Commission have created feeding lawns where they
leave food in winter.

Most fallow are red brown with white spots in
summer, greyer and less spotted in winter. But
there is also a menil colour, which is a pale
version. Mixed with them will be the black (dusky
brown in winter), and sometimes white, which vary
from sandy to cream. Bucks grow to about a yard
high at the shoulder and have "palmate" antlers, a
long wing shape with spikes very different from a
red stag. Fallow have long white tails with a thick
black stripe.

Red deer had long gone from the Chase but two small
herds have been established recently at Beaudesert
and Teddesley. Muntjac are a species introduced to
Woburn Park in Bedfordshire before World War II.
The armed services took over the park for a period,
fences were neglected and the little muntjacs, no
bigger than a dog, slipped out into the fields and
hedgerows. They spread to most of the south and
midlands and live in most woodlands in this region.
You will be lucky to see them because they can hide
in bracken or a bramble patch.

You will be unlucky if you do not catch sight of
some fallow on the Chase, I have seen them on most
visits. But here are two warnings. (1) NEVER touch
a lone fawn, it has not been abandoned but it will
be if you interfere. (2) Drive carefully by day or
night. Deer can break out yards in front of your
car, and each year eighty or so are killed by
traffic. If this doesn't slow you down, think of
the dent caused by 95 kg of fallow buck.

Horsepasture Pools

India Hills

Route (30)

Route (30)

Horsepasture Pools

29

Horsepasture Pools
-
India Hills
(West Route)
1.5 miles   2.5 kms

The Pools are the lowest point
in Beaudesert Park, the
woodland covering the south of
the Chase. India Hills is about
200 feet higher. A walk in the
conifers made pleasant with
beech, there is a pocket sized
quarry.

*

Horsepasture Pools
to India Hills
(West Route)

(1) At crosstracks, put your
back to iron gates & take track
ahead.

(2) At end of pool, round L
bend & on 100yds to take next
track L.

(3) Follow .3 mile to road.

(4) Take track opposite, pass
track R, cross a track & curve
R to take next track L.

(5) Follow appx .6 mile to 3
track junction. Curve L & down
L to cross stream.

(6) Take path, go thro chains &
into wood 100yds, to path L.

ROUTE 30 (Horsepasture Pools
via Upper Longdon)
runs ahead, para (f).
You go AHEAD 150yds etc.

(7) Take path L to iron stile &
road bend.

(8) Go L a few paces to "Chase"
sign & take path opposite.

(9) Head for end of quarry, &
20yds from end, take path L.
Follow up quarry edge, pass
path L, & up to meet main path.

(10) Go L up to crest & 5
tracks junction under 2 sets of
power lines.

India Hills
●
>> OPTIONS <<
Routes 27(a), 28(a) & 30(a)

*

India Hills to
Horsepasture Pools
(West Route)

29

(a) At 5 track junction stand
with steep track running down
on your L. Go ahead a few
paces & take R fork.

(b) Follow down appx 400yds to
small path R. [If you miss you
soon come to quarry edge R. Go
back up 60 paces.]

(c) Follow small path R down &
bend L into quarry.

(d) Go R to road. Cross & go L,
curving R to take iron stile by
house gate.

(e) Follow path into wood &
meet path.

(f) Go R, pass wood barrier, go
thro chains & cross stream.

(g) Follow track up, pass 2
tracks L & follow appx .6 mile
to road.

(h) Take track opposite appx .3
mile to meet track.

ROUTE 30 (India Hills
via Upper Longdon)
runs L, up to iron gates,
then para (3)

(i) Go R & round R bend to
crosstracks by iron gates.

Horsepasture Pools

>> OPTIONS <<
Routes 30(1), 31(1) & 32(a)

(79)

30

Horsepasture Pools - India Hills
(via Upper Longdon)
2.3 miles   3.7 kms

Only this route and numbers (1) and (27) wander off
the Chase. This is an excursion to the village of
Upper Longdon. There is a track in a deep sandstone
holloway, some field paths, and what may be the
finest hilltop view of Rugeley, if that is what you
wanted. Take a look at the ruinous white stucco
lodge near Upper Longdon, it may still be for sale.

*

Horsepasture Pools
to India Hills
(via Upper Longdon)

(1) At crosstracks, put your
back to iron gates, & take
stone track ahead.

(2) Follow L bend round end of
pool, pass track L & curve R up
to iron gates.

(3) Go to R of gates & follow
wood edge path. Exit L to road
at 1st chance.

(4) Cross & go R appx 300yds to
grass island at

Upper Longdon

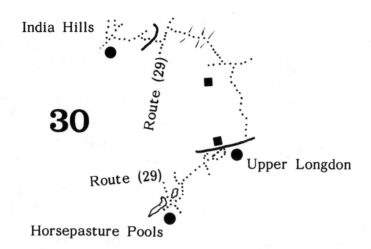

India Hills

Route (29)

30

Route (29)

Upper Longdon

Horsepasture Pools

(5) Take track behind grass island .5 miles, to T junction.

(6) Go L appx 100yds to end of trees R. Bear R upfield 45deg to pass R side of lone tree.

(7) Keep same line & take stile. Go L along hedge & via gates to steep field.

(8) SIGHT fenced track ahead & below. Go down midfield to join it via (? bust) stiles.

(9) Follow fenced path to T junction. Go L 100yds to path R

ROUTE 29 (Horsepasture Pools, West Route)
runs AHEAD to barrier, para (f)

(10) Take path R to iron stile & road bend.

(11) Go L a few paces to Chase sign, & take path opposite.

(12) Head for end of quarry & 20 yds from end, take path L. Follow up quarry edge, pass path L, & up to meet main path.

(13) Go L up to crest & 5 tracks junction under 2 sets of power lines.

India Hills
●
>> OPTIONS <<
Routes 27(a), 28(a) & 30(a)

30

*
India Hills to
Horsepasture Pools
(via Upper Longdon)

(a) At 5 track junction stand with steep track running down on your L. Go ahead a few paces & take R fork.

(b) Follow down appx 400yds to small path R. [If you miss you soon come to quarry edge R. Go back up 60 paces.]

(c) Follow small path R down & bend L into quarry.

(d) Go R to road. Cross & go L, curving R to take iron stile by house gate.

(e) Follow path into wood & meet path.

(f) Go L appx 150yds to gates & go R to take stile.

(g) SIGHT along fenced path to summit & trees. Head for summit via stiles (? bust) & up to gates. ◢

(h) Take gates, go with hedge on your R & take stile R.

(i) SIGHT ahead farm & small building to R. Head for R end of small building. When line of trees ahead is in sight, go down to their R end & track.

(j) Go L to gate & take track R appx .3 mile up to road at

Upper Longdon.

(k) Put grass island on your R & follow road appx 300yds to last house R, "Leighswood".

(l) Cross road. Take SMALL PATH at end of stone drive. Go R, (parallel with drive) to its end. Bear R & join track.

(m) Go ahead & down to L bend & track R.

ROUTE 29 (India Hills West Route)
takes track R, para (3)

(n) Go on round L bend & bend R to crosstracks by iron gates.

Horsepasture Pools
●

>> OPTIONS <<
Routes 29(1), 31(1) & 32(a)

(82)

A nice enough walk through the pines with an
enjoyable muddy bit when it's wet. There is little
to be seen of the pools from any of these routes,
except what you can make out from the
bridge near the iron gates.

31 Horsepasture Pools - Beaudesert .75 mile 1.2 kms

Beaudesert

Horsepasture Pools

Horsepasture Pools to Beaudesert

(1) At crosstracks face iron gates. Go R & take 1st track L.

(2) Follow appx .5 mile up to crosstracks under power lines.

Beaudesert

>> OPTIONS <<
Routes 33(a) & 35(1)

Beaudesert to Horsepasture Pools

(a) At crosstracks, face downhill & take track L.

(b) Follow appx .5 mile & round hairpin bend, to meet track.

(c) Go R to crosstracks by iron gates.
Horsepasture Pools

>> OPTIONS <<
Routes 29(1), 30(1) & 32(a)

32

Castle Ring - Horsepasture Pools
1.1 miles 1.8 kms

The Ring is the highest point on the Chase at about 800 feet, and the Pools are some 400 feet below. This and the views that it commands explain why Iron Age people built their refuge here. Until recently the views were negligable, blocked by mature conifers. Now that the Forestry Commission has cropped them I am hoping for more sensitive new plantings.

Horsepasture Pools

Castle Ring

＊

Castle Ring to
Horsepasture Pools

(1) From car park get onto Ring rampart & go R.

(2) After appx 300yds watch for house R. Go towards it, then L along garden fence to corner.

(3) Go R parallel with fence 75 paces, to where fence from R meets it at godfather posts.

(4) Go L down wide steep path 80 paces, to dip & hump.

(5) NB small valley R; take path above it to meet path. Go L, pass small path L & cross log & spring.

(6) Go ahead, across paths R & L, to path T junction. Go L down clear path to stone track.

(7) Go ahead to junction & ahead to crosstracks by gates.

Horsepasture Pools
●
>> OPTIONS <,
Routes 29(1), 30(1) & 31(1)

(84)

*

Horsepasture Pools
to Castle Ring

(a) At crosstracks FACE iron gates & PASS THEM ON YOUR R, up to junction of stone tracks.

(b) Take stone track ahead to its end. Cross turning area & take steep rising path.

(c) Path gets fainter, keep CLIMBING. Look for wire fence L, & go parallel with it to end

(d) Join Ring rampart & follow R or L to car park.

Castle Ring
●
>> OPTIONS <<
Routes 33(1) & 34(1)

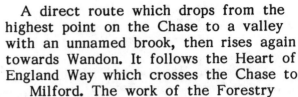

Castle Ring - Beaudesert
.9 mile 1.5 kms

33

A direct route which drops from the highest point on the Chase to a valley with an unnamed brook, then rises again towards Wandon. It follows the Heart of England Way which crosses the Chase to Milford. The work of the Forestry Commission is very obvious, but conifers we have got on the southern Chase, so I appreciate this opportunity to view them as miles of treetops.

Beaudesert

Castle Ring

*

Castle Ring to Beaudesert

(1) From car park, take path passing Ring on your R to meet cross path. Go L to track.

(2) Go down with power lines, over crosstrack, to R bend & fork. Go L & cross stream.

(3) Rise & cross next stream, then on to next crosstracks by power pole.

Beaudesert

●

>> OPTIONS <<
Routes 31(a) & 35(1)

Beaudesert to Castle Ring

(a) From crosstracks go DOWN with power lines & cross valley bottom stream.

(b) Go up to junction, then R. Cross a track, follow power lines to CREST & take track L.

(c) Bear L to Ring rampart & follow R or L to car park.

Castle Ring

●

>> OPTIONS <<
Routes 32(1) & 34(1)

Names on the Chase

Explanations make sense of some place names, which often turn out as mundane as old wellies. Sherbrook is a golden exception. A few remain baffling and probably all the better for it.

Beaudesert; beautiful wild place.

Brereton; briar hill.

Brindley Heath; woodland cleared by burning, also the name of one of the Paget gamekeepers.

Broadhurst Green; a hurst is a hilltop clump of trees, and this was a wide one with a clearing.

Dimmings Dale; Demons Dale -??

Etching Hill; Eychilhill 1504, Ichinhill 1584 Iching Hill 1694, Eachings Hill 1798, Hitching Hill 1834 - goodness knows.

Flaxley Green; a woodland clearing where flax was grown. (You see what I mean about the wellies.)

Gospel Place; on the boundary between the parishes of Brocton and Brindley Heath and named after the Rogation Day ceremony of beating the bounds.

Hagley; wood were haws were found.

..ley, as a name ending; woodland pasture

Moors Gorse; moor or marshland.

Rising Brook; Ryssinbrooke 1584, a stream with its source in brushwood.

Sherbrook; Sherbroke 1290, the shining stream.

Shoal Hill; Le Sholle 1300, Shore Hill 1834, a hill with a twisted shape.

Shropshire Brook; it is miles from the county and flows away from it, probably the name of a tenant.

slade; slad - valley. Hence Deercote Slade - a shelter (cot) for deer. The other slades are pretty obvious - Hazel, Spring etc.

Slitting Mill; a village grew around a mill on the Rising Brook in the 1700's. See the industrial history bit on what slitting might be.

Startley Piece; woodland pasture on a projecting piece of land.

Stile Cop; steep hill (go and see).

Weetman's Bridge over the Trent near Seven Springs replaced a perilous 200 foot timber span in 1888. Joseph Weetman provided most of the cash.

Castle Ring - Golf Club
1.8 miles   3 kms

A level walk on the edge of the woods with oak, beech, hazel and shrubby things softening the pines. Take a good look at the pond and be careful when you get to the road.

34

Golf Club

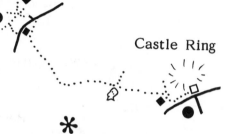

Castle Ring

*

Castle Ring to Golf Club

(1) From car park, exit to road. Face entrance & take path on its L.

(2) Follow WOOD EDGE paths PARALLEL with lane L, to track & house.

(3) Take track past R side of house appx 1.25 miles to road.

GREAT CARE
DO NOT CROSS YET

(4) Go L on verge to house L, then on appx 60 paces.

(5) [CARE] Take track opposite up to meet track. Go R to golf waiting area.

Golf Club
●
>> OPTIONS <<
Routes 23(a) & 24(1)

*

Golf Club to Castle Ring

(a) At golf waiting area, put your back to clubhouse. Go 50 paces with course on your R & take track L to road.

GREAT CARE

(b) Cross NOW & go L ON VERGE to opposite golf club entrance.

(c) Take track R appx 1.25 miles to track & house R.

(d) Take path opposite (para--llel with lane R) to car park.

Castle Ring
●
>> OPTIONS <<
Routes 32(1) & 33(1)

Beaudesert - Lower Cliff
.9 mile 1.5 kms

35

The place I have called Lower Cliff is shown as Seven Springs on the maps, but I could not use that name a second time. There must be springs because you meet another pool on this route, which is otherwise a pleasant but unremarkable wander through the pines.

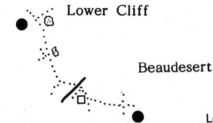

Lower Cliff

Beaudesert

✳

Beaudesert to Lower Cliff

(1) At crosstracks face downhill & take track R appx 400 yds to road.

GREAT CARE

(2) Take track opposite appx 200 yds & fork R. Pass pool R (& tracks L) & on to pool L at T junction.

Lower Cliff
●
>> OPTIONS <<
Routes 25(a), 26(1) & 28(1)

Lower Cliff to Beaudesert

(a) At track junction by pool, take minor track PASSING POOL ON YOUR L.

(b) Pass next pool L (& tracks R) & on to meet track. Go L to road.
GREAT CARE

(c) Enter car park opposite & take track L, angling from road down to crosstracks by power pole.
Beaudesert
●
>> OPTIONS <<
Routes 31(a) & 33(a)